CANADA'S
CONSTITUTIONAL
MONARCHY

The Duke and Duchess of Cambridge participate in a July 1 citizenship ceremony, welcoming new Canadians and handing out flags.
Department of Canadian Heritage.

CANADA'S CONSTITUTIONAL MONARCHY

Nathan Tidridge

DUNDURN
NATURAL HERITAGE
TORONTO

Editor: Allister Thompson
Copy-editor: Shannon Whibbs
Design: Courtney Horner
Printer: Webcom

Library and Archives Canada Cataloguing in Publication

Tidridge, Nathan, 1978-
     Canada's constitutional monarchy / by Nathan Tidridge.

Includes bibliographical references and index.
Issued also in electronic formats.
ISBN 978-1-55488-980-8

     1. Constitutional history--Canada. 2. Monarchy--Canada--
History. 3. Canada--Politics and government. I. Title.

KE4199.T53 2011   342.7102'9   C2011-903791-2
KF4482.T53 2011

1   2   3   4   5   15   14   13   12   11

Conseil des Arts du Canada   Canada Council for the Arts   Canada   ONTARIO ARTS COUNCIL CONSEIL DES ARTS DE L'ONTARIO

We acknowledge the support of the **Canada Council for the Arts** and the **Ontario Arts Council** for our publishing program. We also acknowledge the financial support of the **Government of Canada** through the **Canada Book Fund** and **Livres Canada Books**, and the **Government of Ontario** through the **Ontario Book Publishing Tax Credit** and the **Ontario Media Development Corporation**.

Care has been taken to trace the ownership of copyright material used in this book. The author and the publisher welcome any information enabling them to rectify any references or credits in subsequent editions.

J. Kirk Howard, President

Printed and bound in Canada.
www.dundurn.com

Dundurn
3 Church Street, Suite 500
Toronto, Ontario, Canada
M5E 1M2

Gazelle Book Services Limited
White Cross Mills
High Town, Lancaster, England
LA1 4XS

Dundurn
2250 Military Road
Tonawanda, NY
U.S.A. 14150

Dedicated to my daughters Sophie and Elyse,
as well as all other students of Canada's history and government

An institution that is continually depreciated either by design or ignorance, like the Canadian Crown, will eventually wither and die, and with it an integral part of our constitution.

— Senator Serge Joyal, editor of *Protecting Parliamentary Democracy*, opening the first policy conference on the role of the Crown in Canadian governance. The conference was sponsored by Queen's University (Institute of Intergovernmental Relations) and held on Parliament Hill, June 9–10, 2010.

The insignia worn by Queen Elizabeth II as Sovereign of the Order of Canada. Designed in 1968, this special insignia was presented to the Queen two years later by Governor General Roland Michener. National Defence.

TABLE OF CONTENTS

Acknowledgements   11

Introduction   15

Chapter One: The History of the Crown in Canada   23

Chapter Two: The Canadian Constitution and Authority   54

Chapter Three: The Queen of Canada   70

Chapter Four: The Governor General and the National Crown   81

Chapter Five: The Lieutenant Governors and the Provincial Crowns   94

Chapter Six: The Crown in Day-to-Day Life   103

Chapter Seven: First Nations and the Crown   125

Chapter Eight: The Military and the Crown   141

Chapter Nine: The Canadian Honours System   153

Chapter Ten: The Canadian Heraldic Authority   169

Chapter Eleven: Royal and Vice-Regal Tours   179

Chapter Twelve: The Heir to the Throne   189

Chapter Thirteen: The Commonwealth and the Queen's Other Realms   200

Appendix A: Did You Know?   207

Appendix B: Canadian Sovereigns and their Representatives   233

Appendix C: Officers and Officials of the Crown   240

Appendix D: Titles and Forms of Address   249

Appendix E: Websites   251

Appendix F: Definitions   255

Bibliography   265

Index   271

ACKNOWLEDGEMENTS

I am indebted to many for the help they gave me during this project. My favourite part of this whole process has been meeting with and learning from people across the country. Through these individuals I have grown to appreciate the Canadian Crown even more than when I started this book.

Much time was taken in locating images that would help illustrate the points I needed to make. The assistance of the following made this search both a pleasant and rewarding experience:

Susan R. Bernard, Department of Canadian Heritage

Patrick Berrea, Directorate of Honours and Recognition, Department of National Defence

The Canadian Heraldic Authority

Sergeant Ryan Davidson, Directorate of History and Heritage, Department of National Defence

Hon. Paul Delorey, Speaker of the Legislative Assembly of the Northwest Territories

Adrienne Dunton, Communications and Events Coordinator, Office of the Lieutenant Governor of British Columbia

Caroline Ganon, Senate of Canada

Major Carl Gauthier, Directorate of Honours and Recognition, Department of National Defence

Jane Gibson and Barry Penhale of Natural Heritage Books/Dundurn

The Glenbow Archives

Devon Guest, Canadian Football League

Danielle P. Hawwa, Office of the Law Clerk and Parliamentary Counsel, House of Commons

Fred H. Hayward UE, President of the United Empire Loyalists Association of Canada

Elisabeth Hugel, Registrar of Honours and Awards, Office of the Provincial Secretary, Protocol Office of Saskatchewan

Legislative Assembly of Nunavut

Library and Archives of Canada

Floyd McCormick, Clerk of the Yukon Legislative Assembly

Mélanie McKinnon, Public Works and Government Services Canada

Ruth Nicholson UE

The Office of the Speaker, Ontario Legislature

The Office of the Speaker, Manitoba Legislature

The Office of Ted McMeekin, M.P.P. for Ancaster-Dundas-Flamborough-Westdale

Krista Rodd, Administrative Assistant, Office of the Lieutenant Governor of Prince Edward Island

Constable Paulina Sokoloski, Royal Canadian Mounted Police

It was important to me to present information that was accurate, and I am indebted to the following for looking over sections of this book and offering their insights and suggestions (and providing some excellent images):

Arthur Bousfield, The Canadian Royal Heritage Trust

Rafal Heydel-Mankoo, Editor, Burke's Peerage & Gentry: World Orders of Knighthood and Merit

Dr. D. Michael Jackson, C.V.O., S.O.M., C.D., University of Regina

Darrel Kennedy, Assiniboine Herald, Canadian Heraldic Authority

Lieutenant-Commander Scott Nelson, M.V.O., Canadian Equerry to the Queen (2010 Royal tour)

Dr. David Smith, University of Saskatchewan

Dr. Christopher McCreery, M.V.O., Private Secretary to the Lieutenant Governor of Nova Scotia

Of the people that helped me with my manuscript, I owe the most thanks to Father Jacques Monet, s.j., and Professor Thomas Symons C.C., O.Ont., FRSC., LL.D.

Father Monet kindly sat with me until late one night at the Jesuits' provincial office, poring over several chapters — I am in awe of his knowledge and generosity. I can remember reading Father Monet's book *The Canadian Crown* as a high school student (and I proudly now have my own copy).

Professor Symons was a mentor to me, reading the manuscript from beginning to end over the phone. I was privileged to be a guest of Dr. Symons at the annual Symons Lecture on the state of Confederation held in Charlottetown, Prince Edward Island. For this project, my time at the Symons Lecture was transformative. I am indebted to the kindness Dr. Symons has shown me – he is truly a wise man and great Canadian.

It was as a high school teacher that I approached this topic, and I was honoured to have some former students agree to look over my text. The suggestions offered by Chase Anderson, Nicole Brandt, Brad Farquhar, Zach Hrozjak, Janine Matetich, and Darcy Shea were invaluable to me. It is students like these that make people want to become teachers.

The love and support of my family was key to getting this book done. I owe so much to my wife, Christine Vanderwal, for allowing me to spend so many days and nights reading and writing. Chris is the love of my life, and this whole process has taught me how precious it is to be supported. Thank you.

INTRODUCTION

Canada is a blended family made up of very different provinces, territories, regions, and peoples. These differences can range from language to environment, and just as in any blended family, they can be sources of conflict and misunderstanding. There is always the danger that Ontario's concerns could overshadow those of Nova Scotia, that the rights of one group of people could seem more important than those of another, or that the preservation of one region's culture could be threatened by another's larger population. Every part of Canada brings something different to our national and provincial tables, creating the very complicated country in which we live.

So how do we keep it all together?

Institutions have grown within our country that unite us as Canadians (as well as Albertans, Quebecers, Manitobans, etc.). The most important of these institutions — the very foundation of the entire country — is the Crown.

Canada is a constitutional monarchy with a Parliament made up of the Queen, the Senate, and the House of Commons, as well as thirteen provincial and territorial legislatures.

This means that formal power is vested in a Sovereign, but can only be used by following the rules and unwritten traditions of the constitution of Canada.

The governor general's flag flies at Province House, Prince Edward Island, the birthplace of Confederation. Photo by Nathan Tidridge.

Canadians enjoy one of the most stable forms of government on the planet, but there is a crisis in our understanding of that government, and in particular of the Crown. More than simply an ornament in our political system, the Crown is at the very centre of our constitution and democracy. As Queen of Canada, Elizabeth II personifies the Crown and our democratic traditions. Located outside of politics, the Crown exists to give authority to, and protect, our constitution and government. As explained in the Department of Canadian Heritage publication *A Crown of Maples*:

> In a constitutional monarchy such as Canada's, power does not rest with any one person. Rather, power lies within an institution that functions to safeguard it on behalf of all its citizens. That institution is the Crown.

Prince Charles wears a pair of the famous Hudson's Bay Company Olympic red mittens in the lead-up to the 2010 Winter Games. The Prince is pictured with then-premier of British Columbia, Gordon Campbell. Department of Canadian Heritage.

Canada is also a Confederation — a union of different provinces into one state. Not only does the monarch embody the Canadian State, but also the sovereignty of each individual province. The Crown provides the structure needed to allow all of Canada's different regions and peoples' to live together peacefully. This is no small task.

Canadian philosopher Charles Taylor wrote that individuals need events and people that can serve as fixed points at which they can stand and say "This is who we are." The

Queen acts as the main fixed point of our society — not representing one particular group or region, but rather the entire country or province.

In 1976, a comprehensive survey from across the country by the Commission on Canadian Studies was released. Headed by Professor T.H. Symons, the commission was asked to "study, report, and make recommendations upon the state of teaching and research in various fields of study relating to Canada." Symons's report, titled *To Know Ourselves*, was far-reaching, highlighting real concerns about the formation of a Canadian identity:

> Unless Canadians recognize their distinctiveness in time and place, and are sufficiently interested in themselves and in their society and country, what motivation is there for self-study? The perception of Canadian identity may differ markedly from person to another, from one language or cultural group to another, and from one part of the country to another. But an awareness of being Canadian, and an interest in the nature of that condition, is necessary for the achievement of self-knowledge; for what is self-knowledge, as far as a Canadian is concerned, if not the knowledge of one's identity?

The commission focused on many different areas of education, including the initiatives being taken or not taken around Canada's political system, and its conclusions were a cause for concern:

> While lacking adequate opportunities to learn about their own political system, Canadian students are subjected by the media to a mass of information about the American political system. By the time they enter university, in fact, many of them have been conditioned to think almost completely in terms of American political ideals, terminology, institutions and practices. They have simply not learned that the Canadian political system differs substantially from that of the United States or, indeed, of any other country. University teachers in every part of Canada told the Commission that even some of their final-year students do not know the

distinction, for example, between the Canadian parliamentary system and the American congressional system, between the role and responsibilities of the Prime Minister of Canada and those of the President of the United States, between the powers of a Canadian Provincial Lieutenant-Governor and those of an American State Governor ...

Sadly, such conclusions are still true today, thirty-five years after this pivotal report. The report's conclusion that "... no student should be permitted to graduate from high school, and still less from university, without certain minimal levels of knowledge about the political institutions and political culture of this country" has not been heard.

In the Ontario curriculum there is no mention of the words Sovereign/monarch/Queen, governor general, prime minister, Cabinet, or responsible government within the Grade 10 Civics document (the only time government is discussed in high school). The definition — wholly incorrect — of parliament is given as: "An elected assembly responsible for passing legislation and granting the right to levy taxes. In Canada, the federal legislature consists of the Sovereign's representative, the Senate, and the House of Commons." While the definition is given in the document's glossary, there is no mandate that it must be learned by the students. The absence of such key fundamentals of Canada's political structure holds true in the curricula of Nova Scotia, Saskatchewan, Alberta, and Quebec, while Newfoundland and Labrador, Manitoba, British Columbia (although the Sovereign is not mentioned), Prince Edward Island do deal with them to varying degrees.

In an article published in 2010 by *Maclean's* magazine, John Fraser (master of Massey College, University of Toronto) points out that the plight of Prince Charles as heir to the throne is symptomatic of Canada's treatment of the institution of the Crown. Fraser wrote "He is a warm-hearted, decent and thoughtful man who has espoused causes that are dear to many Canadians' hearts and did so long before they were popular, particularly on the ecological and climate change fronts, but also with his concerns for the quality of life for ordinary people." Still, the heir to the Canadian throne has been kept absent from our national life (his 2009 tour was the first in eight years).

Partly thanks to the recent wedding and historic Royal tour of the Duke and Duchess of Cambridge, as well as the Queen's Diamond Jubilee in 2012, there has been a resurgence of interest concerning our constitutional monarchy. Running up against this engagement are decades of neglect and misinformation. Without proper education and understanding, it is no wonder that whenever Canadians encounter the monarchy, they are confused. The governor general is often referred to by the media as the Canadian head of state, while the Queen is almost always identified as the British Monarch (even though the principle of a distinct "Canadian Crown" has been evolving since the establishment of responsible government in 1848, and the Queen was distinctly named "Queen of Canada" by the Royal Styles and Titles Act of 1953). Almost uniformly, these errors are echoed in school textbooks and curricula across the country. Even government (both federal and provincial) publications routinely cast the Crown as merely a symbolic institution with no impact on the day-to-day lives of Canadians. This is simply not true. As we move into the seventh decade of the reign of Queen Elizabeth II, a looming crisis of identity is beginning to emerge. Over the past decades, a popular disconnect between the Canadian public and the Queen of Canada has been allowed to emerge — a distance created by a lack of understanding that has been fostered (intentionally or otherwise) by educators, public servants, and the media.

The end result is that many Canadians no longer see a direct relationship between the Sovereign and the governor general. Such a perception is not only incorrect, but runs counter to the very idea of representative government first practised in Nova Scotia in 1758. The office of governor general was never meant to be that of a president, and even a modest understanding of our parliamentary traditions makes that very clear. Thankfully, the current governor general is working to reverse this trend, and routinely identifies himself as the personal representative of the Queen of Canada.

The decision to be a constitutional monarchy was made unanimously by delegates at the 1864 Charlottetown Conference, at the very beginning of the story of Canada. Meeting at the time of the American Civil War, the Fathers of Confederation were also mindful that constitutional monarchy was one of the fundamental institutions that set the emerging Canadian state apart from the republic to the south. T.H. Symons explains in *The Landscapes of Confederation* that the Fathers of Confederation consciously chose our form of government:

In an effort to better educate students about their government, many schools are adopting the parliamentary model for their student governments. The Honourable David C. Onley, lieutenant governor of Ontario (left), watches as a mace is presented by his aide-de-camp to Principal Helen McGregor for the Student Parliament of Waterdown District High School in 2007. The school's sergeant-at-arms, Griffin Elliot (far right) stands ready to take the mace while Travis Gourlay acts as the student aide-de-camp. Photo by Jan Jaster.

... while they had no wish to sever ties of affection and allegiance to the Crown, the delegates were not a group of expats yearning over nostalgic memories of the Mother Country. On the contrary, they were strongly rooted and well-established in their respective communities with no wish to be elsewhere.

This book has been written to to introduce them to a rich institution that is integral to our ideas of democracy and parliamentary government. Vetted by experts from across the country, *Canada's Constitutional Monarchy* joins such publications as Kevin MacLeod's *Crown of Maples* (2008), Michael Jackson's *The Canadian Monarchy in Saskatchewan* (1990), Jacques Monet's *The Canadian Crown* (1979), and Frank McKinnon's *The Crown in Canada* (1976) in explaining a complex, ancient, and thoroughly Canadian institution.

As Carl Sandburg once said "When a society or civilization perishes, one constant can always be found: they forgot where they came from."

Nathan Tidridge
Carlisle, Ontario
2011

Chapter One

THE HISTORY OF THE CROWN IN CANADA

There was a reason that the Fathers of Confederation wanted to call their new country "The Kingdom of Canada." Even though it was the British government that ultimately vetoed the name (fearing it would upset the Americans), the Crown has been fixed within the Canadian system of government since Europeans landed on the shores of Newfoundland and Gaspé centuries ago.

"No part of this country has ever been a republic or part of a republic and to become one would be an abrupt break with our history," wrote the late Senator Eugene Forsey. "Our monarchy, our British monarchy, our Anglo-French monarchy, our historic monarchy, is part of the Canadian tradition. It is not something alien. It is bone of our bone and flesh of our flesh."

Sailing for the English Crown, Giovanni Caboto claimed the new lands to the west, or the "new found land," for Henry VII in 1497. South of Newfoundland, Jacques Cartier landed in Gaspé in 1534 to declare the vast region surrounding the St. Lawrence under the authority of French King François I.

Soon after, the history of these lands became filled with stories of conflict between the English and French, as well as the First Peoples who were forced to deal with them. First Nations and early settlers (such as the Acadians) found their lands change hands from English to French, and back again, a number of times. It is this history, as well as the relationships European settlers had with the Aboriginal peoples, that has shaped how we are now governed.

Surrounded by courtiers, King François I receives Jacques Cartier and hears his stories of discoveries in the west. This painting is one of six by Frank Craig (1874–1918) produced as illustrations for The King's Book of Québec, *published in Ottawa by Mortimer Co. Limited, 1911. Library and Archives of Canada, 1996-23-1.*

Throughout this time there have been pivotal events that shaped what Canada's government would look like, but it is important to remember that the country we now know only came together in 1867. Before Confederation, the various British and French colonies of North America saw themselves as separate and unique places, independent from each other. This early history of separation explains why today's provinces remain so protective of their local identities and governments.

The following are some events that explain the role of the Crown in the development of Canada as a modern state.

QUEEN ELIZABETH I AND HER EXPLORERS, 1576–1603

With Queen Elizabeth I waving her neckerchief from a window at Greenwich Palace, English explorer Martin Frobisher set out in 1576 on what would become a series of expeditions to the high Arctic of North America in search of a Northwest Passage to China. After returning from his first voyage with samples of ore he believed contained gold, Frobisher founded the Company of Cathay and made plans to set out the following spring with the support (both moral and financial) of his Sovereign. During his second voyage, Frobisher landed on modern-day Baffin Island, claiming it in the name of the Queen. Frobisher's third voyage ended in financial ruin as the "gold" he mined out of the Arctic turned out to be worthless pyrite and all attempts to colonize ended in failure. Still, the explorer had sparked an interest in his Queen to establish a vast northern empire in the continent.

Royal Arms of New France. The three lilies, called "French Modern" by people familiar with heraldry, represent the Roman Catholic belief in the Father, Son, and Holy Ghost. These particular arms came from Fortress of Louisburg and were saved from destruction by Governor General The Earl of Dufferin (1872–78). CWM 19940024-001. © Canadian War Museum.

Elizabeth I turned to other explorers including Sir Humphrey Gilbert, who tried to establish a colony on Newfoundland in 1583, and Sir Walter Raleigh, who founded the infamous settlement at Roanoke Island (off the coast of present-day Virginia). Both schemes ended in failure, but signalled the renewed interest of the English Crown (with its financial resources) in North America, which would continue beyond the reign of the Virgin Queen.

HENRI IV, KING OF FRANCE, 1589–1610

After Cartier's famous voyages, very little was done to promote French interests in North America until the reign of King Henri IV. Actively engaged in the settlement and development of New France, Henri IV's vision was heavily influenced by the recent European wars of religion. The French King saw the new world as a community of Protestants and Roman Catholics loyal to the same crown and governed by a nobility based on merit and virtue. King Henri's drive ensured the settlement of New France, capturing the imaginations of such explorers as Samuel de Champlain (who shared a similar vision for North America).

———————

AYMAR DE CHASTE — CANADA'S FIRST VICEROY, 1602

King Henri IV appointed de Chaste, a man who shared his vision of a place of religious tolerance and harmony, as viceroy of Canada in 1602. Nearing the end of his career, de Chaste was highly respected and very well connected. It was Aymar de Chaste that Samuel de Champlain approached to become involved with the development of New France. With this meeting, author David Hackett Fischer wrote in *Chaplain's Dream:*

> … the elements came together. Aymar de Chaste … was a leader with a large spirit who won the respect and affection of all who knew him. Champlain was the junior partner, but with the ear of the king and his strong support. Henri IV was the royal patron who contributed his own broad vision, energy and resolve. As a group, these men framed a great enterprise that combined exploration, trade and settlement.

———————

SAMUEL DE CHAMPLAIN, (INVOLVED WITH CANADA FROM 1602 TO 1635)

Samuel de Champlain's involvement with Canada began when King Henri IV accepted his request to join Aymar De Chaste's expedition to North America. In total, Champlain travelled to New France twenty-seven times during his career, often as the representative of the French Viceroy (who, with the exception of Pierre Dugua, sieur de Mons, stayed at court in France). Champlain brought with him the vision of Henri IV and worked with the First Nations he encountered. The great settlements at Port Royal (1605, modern-day Annapolis Royal) and Quebec City (1608) were founded by the explorer as he travelled as far west as the Great Lakes. Champlain lobbied tirelessly for projects in New France, particularly after the death of King Henri IV and the accession of Louis XIII.

The rise of the powerful Cardinal Richelieu (King Louis XIII's first minister since 1624) saw the creation in 1627 of the Hundred Associates (a.k.a the Company of New France) who held a monopoly on trade and settlement in New France. The Cardinal, as the head of this monopoly, became the ruler of New France (in the name of the King). As with previous viceroys, Richelieu deputized Champlain as his lieutenant.

After briefly losing New France to the English during a war from 1628 to 1629 (which included his capture at Quebec three months after the treaty ending the conflict had been signed), Champlain was returned to the territory in 1632 as acting governor. Samuel de Champlain died in Quebec on December 25, 1635, after suffering a stroke.

Today's governors general trace the roots of their role as the personal representative of the Sovereign in Canada all the way back to Champlain, making it the oldest Canadian public office in existence.

Louis XIV as a young man, *Edmond Lechevallier-Chevignard (1825–1902), artist. Library and Archives of Canada, C-107650.*

ABSOLUTE MONARCHY AND THE SOVEREIGN COUNCIL, 1663

King Louis XIV ("The Sun King") placed New France under his direct control as a Royal province (*province de France*) under the close watch of his minister of the marine, Jean-Baptiste Colbert. King Louis established a "Sovereign

Council" to make laws and hear criminal and civil cases in New France. At the head of the table sat three people: the Governor (representative of the King), the Intendant (official responsible for justice, public order and finance), and the Bishop of Quebec.

HUDSON'S BAY COMPANY, CREATED BY ROYAL CHARTER, 1670

Following the ill-fated explorations of Henry Hudson in 1610, North America's oldest company was created under the patronage of British King Charles II's cousin Prince Rupert in 1670. The Royal Charter issued by the King granted the vast Hudson Bay watershed to a "… Company of Adventurers of England trading into Hudson Bay." Nearly one-third of North America came into the possession of a company eager to feed the European hunger for fur. The Hudson's Bay Company had a tremendous influence on British North America (including the colonies of Vancouver Island and British Columbia), and it is from its great holdings that the provinces of Manitoba, Saskatchewan, and Alberta would be carved, as well as the Yukon, Northwest Territories and, most recently, Nunavut.

ACADIANS AND THE TREATY OF UTRECHT, 1713

The French distinguished the two main regions of New France as *Canada* (denoting the St. Lawrence Valley) and *Acadia* (the eastern, or maritime areas). France's interests were largely with Canada, and so Acadia was often ignored, or used as a bargaining chip during negotiations in Europe. During the conclusion of Queen Anne's War (a.k.a. The War of the Spanish Succession), the French Crown transferred the territory of Acadia (including its inhabitants) to the British Crown. Renamed Nova Scotia, Acadia was often looked at with suspicion by British officials, especially since the French Crown retained nearby Île Royal (Cape Breton Island) which became home to the Fortress of Louisbourg in 1720. By 1717, Acadians had declared their neutrality in the face of any renewed conflicts between the British and French. In 1730, the British Crown

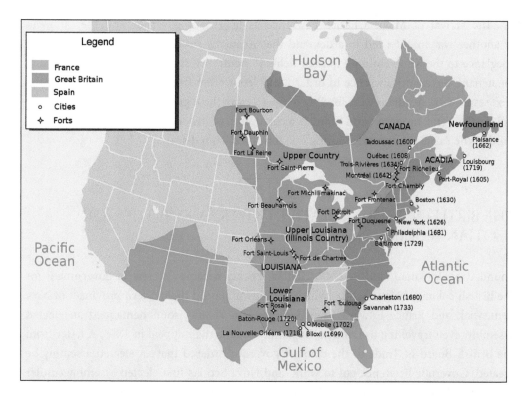

North America after the Treaty of Utrecht. Map by Pinpin.

required Acadians to make the following oath, in exchange for religious freedom and the right to maintain their neutrality: "I sincerely promise and swear on my faith as a Christian that I will be utterly loyal, and will truly obey His Majesty King George the second, whom I recognize as the Sovereign lord of Acadia or Nova Scotia. May God so help me."

Tensions between the British and French in Europe led to King George's War (1744–1748), which saw the capture of the Fortress of Louisbourg by New Englanders. The 1748 peace treaty returned the fortress to the French Crown (outraging the American colonials and laying the groundwork for the 1776 revolution), causing the British to look at Nova Scotia with a new interest. Thousands of colonists (largely Protestants to counter the Acadian Roman Catholics) were brought into the colony as the capital was moved from Annapolis Royal to the newly established port of Halifax.

The arrival of Major Charles Lawrence as lieutenant governor and the outbreak of another war in 1754 led to a demand that Acadians swear an unconditional oath of allegiance to the King. Holding to their belief in neutrality, the Acadians refused, causing Lieutenant Governor Lawrence to order their deportation from all British lands. For the next seven years Acadians were forcibly removed from the region to be resettled as far away as Louisiana (the modern word *Cajun* is a corruption of *Acadian*). It is estimated that one-third of the Acadians deported during this time died from disease.

THE BIRTH OF REPRESENTATIVE GOVERNMENT: THE NOVA SCOTIAN ASSEMBLY, 1758

Founded on Mi'kmaq land in 1749, Halifax quickly became the seat of government for the British colony of Nova Scotia (which also encompassed the modern provinces of New Brunswick and Prince Edward Island). Settlers in Halifax soon demanded an elected assembly, even travelling to London, England, to make their appeal in 1758. A letter from the British Board of Trade to the colony's governor ordered that an elected assembly be created. Governor Lawrence got to work, and Nova Scotia's first elected assembly (under the Crown) held elections in July 1758. This assembly was the first of its kind in what would become Canada.

THE FRENCH AND INDIAN WARS (A.K.A. THE SEVEN YEARS' WAR AND *LA GUERRE DE LA CONQUÊTE*), 1754–1763

Some call this the first true "world war" because it involved many countries and their territories throughout the world. At the war's centre were the French and British battling for control of the world's resources and shipping lanes.

In North America, the war centred around the Ohio Valley and there was a rush of English settlers into land claimed by the French Crown. Both sides claimed land south of Lake Ontario (some expeditions for the British Crown were led by a then-little known officer named George Washington). Soon tensions spilled over into conflict as Europeans partnered with their First Nations' allies — the Iroquois Confederacy fought with the British Crown while the majority of First Nations sided with the French.

For Canada, the war reached its peak on September 13, 1759, on the Plains of Abraham outside the walls of Quebec City. Ten thousand soldiers under the commands of Major-General Wolfe (British) and General Montcalm (French) fought in a brief battle that saw the deaths of both men, as well as the defeat of the French forces protecting Quebec City.

On September 8, 1760, the Marquess de Vaudreuil (as governor of New France) surrendered to the British Lord Amherst in Montreal, ending the French Empire in North America. The territories and settlers that had formally been under French control were signed over to the British Crown in the Treaty of Paris of 1763. The reign of French Kings over North American territory came to an end (with the exception of two small islands — St. Pierre and Miquelon — off the coast of Newfoundland). With the signing of the Treaty of Paris, the region's last French monarch, Louis XV, was replaced by King George III.

Pierre de Rigaud de Vaudreuil de Cavagnial, Marquis de Vaudreuil (1698–1778), Donat Nonotte (1708–85), artist. The painting was completed before the Marquis was appointed governor general of New France in 1755. Library and Archives of Canada, R3938-1.

KING GEORGE III'S ROYAL PROCLAMATION OF 1763

Please also see Chapter Eight: First Nations and the Crown
The question of what to do with the conquered French territory of North America (which

The Armorial Bearings granted to the United Empire Loyalists on March 8, 1972, highlights their loyalty to the Crown. Notice that one of the weapons depicted on the shield is a tomahawk, highlighting the First Nations Loyalists. The swords represent the Loyalist populations of the original Thirteen Colonies. United Empire Loyalist Association of Canada.

extended into the Mississippi Valley) was addressed by this Royal Proclamation, issued by King George III, in 1763. Under the authority of the Crown, a new jurisdiction — Quebec — was carved out of the vast lands taken from the French. King George's new French subjects were allowed religious freedom and land rights (later expanded by the Quebec Act of 1774).

First Nations' allies of the British were placed under the protection of the Crown, creating a strong relationship between the two as the proclamation became the first recognition of First Nations' rights. The Royal Proclamation stopped all westward expansion into First Peoples' lands by the American Thirteen Colonies, making the King protector of the Natives living there. From this point on, settlers had to go through the Crown in order to acquire Native lands. While originally only applying to the First Nations within the new province of Quebec, the Royal Proclamation has become part of Canada's constitution and continues to be the foundation of a complex relationship between the Canadian government and the majority of the country's Aboriginal peoples.

Called the "Magna Carta" of Canada's First Peoples, the Royal Proclamation tied many of the Native Peoples to the Crown. However, the pronouncement also angered King George III's American colonists who now found themselves closed off from the valuable lands to the west.

THE AMERICAN REVOLUTION AND THE LOYALISTS, 1776–1783

Tensions between the American Colonists and the British Crown erupted into open rebellion in 1776. Quickly, the anger felt by the colonists focused on King George III (it was in his name that all laws were made), and each of the Thirteen Colonies declared its independence from the Crown. Not everyone believed in separation (approximately one-third supported the Crown, one third supported the Continental Congress, and the final third were ambivalent), causing a great number (called "Loyalists") to head north for British territory outside of the Thirteen Colonies.

These Loyalists came from a variety of different backgrounds: English, Irish, Scottish, Dutch, German, Scandinavian, Black (both free and slaves), as well as many Americans born in the Thirteen Colonies. This influx of settlers created new homes for themselves in modern-day Nova Scotia and New Brunswick (settling on land that had been vacated by the Acadians), Quebec and Ontario, where their descendants continue to be active members of their communities. Representatives of the Crown, notably John Graves Simcoe (the first lieutenant governor of Upper Canada), began to mould these regions to reflect a very British identity.

Native allies of the British (largely Mohawk, Cayuga, and Onondaga) made up nearly six thousand of the Loyalists travelling north to safety. The Royal Proclamation of 1763 had created a vast territory for First Nations' peoples to live in west of the Adirondacks, but as the Thirteen Colonies threw off the British Crown, such agreements became obsolete. Fighting alongside the Crown, First Nations' peoples immigrated north to lands set aside for their settlement after the defeat of British forces. The loyalty of the First Nations received special recognition from the Crown (see Chapter Seven).

Twice Americans tried to invade Canada, occupying both Montreal and Quebec City in 1775, but were pushed back. That the republicans were repelled highlights how many French Canadians saw that liberties granted to them by the Crown could only be guaranteed through its continued existence on the continent, for without the Crown, the French would become an unprotected minority.

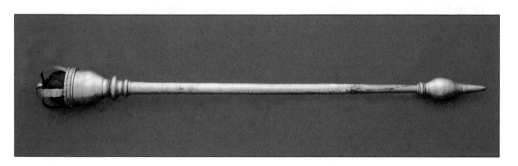

The first mace, used by the Legislature of Upper Canada at Newark in 1792, was captured by American forces in 1812 and not returned to the legislature until 1934 after a goodwill order by President F.D. Roosevelt and the United States Congress. Office of the Speaker of the Ontario Legislature.

In 1783, the independence of the United States of America was officially recognized by the British. A republic (a country not ruled by a king or queen) now existed in North America. The territories (Quebec, Nova Scotia, Prince Edward Island, and Newfoundland) to the north of the American Republic still remained loyal to the British Crown.

————————

ARRIVAL OF PRINCE EDWARD, DUKE OF KENT, 1791–1820

The future father of Queen Victoria arrived in Quebec City as colonel of the Royal Fusiliers, 7th Regiment of Foot, in 1791. This posting began a relationship between the Duke and Canada that lasted long after he permanently left the continent in 1800. Arriving the same year Quebec was split into Upper and Lower Canada, the Duke of Kent toured the Canadas and their major settlements with his Canadienne mistress, Thérèse-Bernardine de Mongenet — a.k.a. Madame St. Laurent. Returning east, the Duke travelled through Montreal while it was holding its first elections for the newly created assembly.

Observing events at Charlesbourg polling station, the Duke addressed (in French) an angry crowd after individuals had been prevented from casting their votes, saying:

> I urge you to unanimity and concord. Let me hear no more of the odious distinction of English and French. You are all His Britannick Majesty's beloved Canadian subjects.

Historian Arthur Bousfield points out that the Duke of Kent's speech:

> … was the first definition of "Canadian" in its modern sense. Before that Canadian meant *Canadien*, a French-speaking native of Quebec. The duke declared a Canadian was an inhabitant of the Canadas, Upper and Lower, whether English-speaking or French-speaking, who was a subject of the King.

Prince Edward,
the Duke of Kent
*(1767–1820), S. Weaver
artist. The original,
painted in Halifax in
1796, hangs in the Nova
Scotia Legislative Library.*
Communications Nova Scotia.

Settling first in Quebec City, the Duke of Kent ultimately took up residence in Halifax in 1793 as commander of the Royal forces in the colony (as well as those of New Brunswick). The Duke of Kent's time in Nova Scotia is often looked upon as a "golden age," and many of the buildings and innovations of this era are connected to him including the first telegraph signal system built in North America. The Duke kept his position as commander-in-chief of North America until 1802, and St. John's Island changed its name to Prince Edward Island in a show of gratitude for his service to the colonies.

In 1814, the Duke wrote a letter to Jonathan Sewell, secretary of the Executive Council of Lower Canada (Canada East), suggesting that the remaining British North American colonies be united together in some sort of union. This letter would be cited by the Fathers of Confederation during their discussions at the Charlottetown Conference of 1864.

THE WAR OF 1812

Understanding this conflict's importance depends on which side of the Canadian-American border you are looking from. Americans see the War of 1812 as their final confrontation with the British in order to secure their independence. Canadians, on the other hand, look at this war as a prime example of American thirst for more territory. Both sides claimed victory even though the boundaries between both countries didn't move. For the northern British colonies, the war served to strengthen the role of the Crown as a rallying point for those weary of American claims for more territory. Even those settlers who were not Loyalists began to see the region's identity firmly intertwined with the British Crown.

RESPONSIBLE GOVERNMENT (A CANADIAN INNOVATION AND KEYSTONE OF OUR DEMOCRATIC TRADITIONS), 1848

Please also see Chapter Two: The Canadian Constitution and Authority

The idea of "responsible government" has evolved over time. Beginning at the end of the Seven Years' War, problems existed between the French and British peoples of British North America. A constant balancing act ensued, and many different models were created to govern these regions. The most dramatic of these models was the Constitution Act of 1791, splitting the province of Quebec into the predominantly English Upper Canada and French Lower Canada.

Power in the Upper and Lower Canadian legislatures was largely exercised by the Crown's representatives (the governors) and their appointed councils (as opposed to the elected assemblies). The Upper and Lower Canada rebellions (1837–1838) highlighted that such rule was not working and a new formula called "responsible government," advocated by Canadians in both Upper and Lower Canada since the early 1820s, was needed:

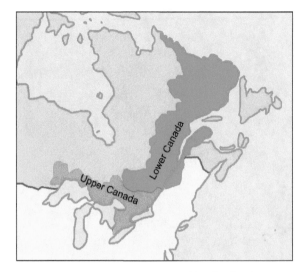

Canada after the Constitution Act of 1791, highlighting the division of the province of Quebec into Upper and Lower Canada.

The basic principles of responsible government:

1. The governor is bound to follow the advice of his executive council.
2. The council should be made up of people that hold the confidence of (meaning: are able to politically control, or command a majority of the votes of) the elected legislature.

Lord Durham's 1838 *Report on the Affairs of British North America* produced a "shot-gun wedding," uniting Upper and Lower Canada under the Union Act of 1840 as one province with a single legislature that moved from settlement to settlement. Neither English nor French Canada was happy with the Union Act, and people began calling for a dramatic shift in government. Led by Robert Baldwin and Louis LaFontaine, Canadians began demanding responsible government that would see the governor choose their "advisors" (the executive council) from a popularly elected assembly. Responsible government was the uniquely Canadian solution to balancing American republicanism with British monarchism.

Joseph Howe, circa 1871, photographer unknown. Howe served as the Queen's representative of Nova Scotia for one month in 1873, from May 10 until his death on June 1. Library and Archives of Canada, C-022002.

The colony of Nova Scotia became the first legislature in the British Empire to practise responsible government. As early as the beginning of the 1830s, Joseph Howe argued for the adoption of responsible government in Nova Scotia — echoing the calls of Robert Baldwin and Louis LaFontaine in the united province of Canada. On January 24, 1848, the Legislative Assembly informed the lieutenant governor of Nova Scotia that:

… we feel that in the course it may be advisable to pursue, with reference to measures so intimately connected with the interests of the people, it is essential to the satisfactory result of our deliberations on these and other matters of public concern, that Her Majesty's Executive Council should enjoy the confidence of the Country; and we consider it our humble duty respectfully to state, that the present Executive Council does not possess that confidence so essential to the promoting of the public welfare, and so necessary to insure to Your Excellency the harmonious co-operation of this Assembly.

On February 9, 1848, the first Nova Scotian Cabinet was selected from members of the Legislative Assembly — the first instance of responsible government in the British Empire. It was this moment that a distinctly Canadian Crown began as the lieutenant governor was now bound to follow the advice of representatives of the local population.

Such a shift did not happen overnight in the province of Canada, but slowly the powers exercised by the governor were transferred to elected representatives who commanded the confidence of (meaning: could control the vote of) the locally elected legislature.

VANCOUVER ISLAND AND BRITISH COLUMBIA, 1849–1858

In an effort to secure British claims to the northwestern coast of the continent in the face of American expansion, the Hudson's Bay Company (who had been granted rights to trade in the region by the Crown) was given a Royal Grant by Queen Victoria to colonize and govern Vancouver Island.

James Douglas became governor of Vancouver Island in 1851, and the following year his jurisdiction was expanded to include the Queen Charlotte Islands (present-day Haida Gwaii). Once gold was discovered in the lower Fraser River, an influx of Americans descended on the region (especially since the Californian gold rush had long since peaked). Governor Douglas claimed the mainland (dubbed "British Columbia" by Queen Victoria) in the name of the Crown, becoming its governor (a separate office) in 1858.

Nova Scotia's flag is actually a banner of the arms granted to the colony by King Charles I in 1625.

THE CRADLE OF CONFEDERATION: THE CHARLOTTETOWN CONFERENCE, 1864

Originally called by the lieutenant governors of New Brunswick, Nova Scotia, and Prince Edward Island to discuss a maritime union, the Canadians (Canada East and West) were invited to come as observers. Situated in Charlottetown, the conference had few hopes, especially since it was competing with the Slaymaker and Nichols Circus (the first to visit the island in twenty-two years). As explained in *The Landscapes of Confederation*:

… the Charlottetown Conference wasn't really supposed to be about Confederation, it wasn't really supposed to be a conference, and it only convened in Charlottetown because Island delegates would not attend otherwise.

Newfoundlanders were invited too late to attend, and there was little to no fanfare to greet the delegates as they arrived. It was the Canadian delegation, headed by co-premiers John A. Macdonald (Canada West) and George-Étienne Cartier (Canada East) that captured the delegates' interests in a union of the remaining British colonies of North America into a new federal state.

———

The delegates to the 1864 Charlottetown Conference sit outside Government House.
Library and Archives of Canada, C-000733.

THE QUEBEC CONFERENCE, 1864

While the idea of Confederation had been agreed upon, the details still needed to be hammered out at another conference held a month later in Quebec (Canada East). The Quebec Conference was not as jovial as the one in Charlottetown, since the delegates had real concerns that needed to be addressed. Newfoundland was in attendance this time, but ultimately the representatives walked away from the negotiating table, along with, ironically, Prince Edward Island.

It was at the Quebec Conference that the idea of a federation was hammered out (keeping in mind the devastating Civil War being conducted in the United States). At the centre of this federation would be the Crown, which George-Étienne Cartier called an "essential element" of the constitution. It was Cartier's Canadian counterpart, Sir John A. Macdonald, who introduced the following motion at the conclusion of the conference:

Prince Edward Island's Government House in 2010. The building remains the official residence of the province's lieutenant governor. Photo *by Nathan Tidridge.*

The Great Seal of Canada, depicting an enthroned Queen Victoria, was used from 1869 through to 1904 (three years after the Sovereign's death). Library and Archives of Canada, Acc. No. 1979-58-15.

The best interest and present and future prosperity of British North America will be promoted by a Federal union under the Crown of Great Britain, provided such union can be affected on principles just to the several provinces.

It was during this conference that the delegates unanimously agreed that the new country would remain a monarchy, with Queen Victoria as its Sovereign.

THE LONDON CONFERENCE AND THE BRITISH NORTH AMERICA ACT, 1866–1867

It was at this conference, also named the Westminster Conference (after the Westminster Arms Hotel) that the final touches were put on a bill by the Canadian delegation to create a new country within the British Empire. John A. Macdonald advocated that Canada be proclaimed a "kingdom" in its own right, but British authorities were concerned that this term was premature and would antagonize the Americans. It was New Brunswick delegate Sir Samuel Leonard Tilley who came up with the name "dominion" (inspired by Psalms 72, verse 8: "He shall have Dominion also from sea to sea, and from the river unto the ends of the earth").

On March 29, 1867, Queen Victoria gave Royal Assent to the British North America Act (since renamed the Constitution Act, 1867) proclaiming the bill to take effect at noon on July 1 that same year. The first words spoken by John A. Macdonald to Queen Victoria after the passage of the British North America Act emphasized that the purpose of Confederation was "… to declare in the most solemn and emphatic manner our resolve to be under the Sovereignty of Your Majesty and your family forever."

At the beginning, only four provinces made up the young dominion: Ontario, Quebec, Nova Scotia, and New Brunswick. More provinces would come, but only after much negotiation and debate.

The Dominion of Canada,
July 1, 1867–July 15,
1870.

DOMINION OF CANADA PURCHASES RUPERT'S LAND, 1870

It was concerns over American expansion into the region that accelerated Canada's acquisition of the vast lands owned by the Hudson's Bay Company. With its charter up for renewal, the Hudson's Bay Company was being criticized by British parliamentarians for keeping their territory undeveloped and largely unsettled. Studies were conducted, and ultimately the HBC charter was not renewed (although the company was permitted to continue its operations). The outbreak of the American Civil War raised fears that once the conflict was over, the United States would march their soldiers north to claim the largely empty Rupert's Land.

It was the Crown that provided the framework for such a purchase to take place as the Hudson's Bay Company agreed to sell the land for $1.5 million to the Canadian government, which would take out a loan from the British government.

Queen Victoria signed the order-in-council that increased Canada's size by ten times. This new territory, called the Northwest Territories, would eventually give birth to the provinces of Alberta, Saskatchewan, and Manitoba, as well as the territories of the Yukon and Nunavut.

————

TRANSFER TO CANADA OF THE ARCTIC ARCHIPELAGO, 1880

The Canadian government was surprised to learn that when they acquired Rupert's Land it did not include the archipelago of islands of the Arctic Ocean. Governor General Lord Dufferin broke the news to the Dominion government after receiving confidential memos from the British Colonial Office. American expansionists were now eyeing the Arctic Archipelago and the Northwest Passage they encompassed, and the Canadian government had to act. On July 31, 1880, Queen Victoria signed an order-in-council that transferred the vast archipelago from her British government to her Canadian. Alan Cooke of McGill University is often quoted as saying that with the stroke of a pen, Canada became the world's second-largest country. Once again, the Crown provided the framework for a peaceful transfer of territory from one government to the other. This event is also one of the foundations of Canada's claim of Arctic sovereignty.

————

LIQUIDATORS OF THE MARITIME BANK OF CANADA V. THE RECEIVER GENERAL OF NEW BRUNSWICK, 1892

This dispute between the government of New Brunswick and the Maritime Bank of Canada clarified the role of the provincial lieutenant governors. Until 1892, lieutenant governors were seen by many as representatives of the federal government within a province and that the only representative of the monarch was the governor general. It was the British Judicial Committee of the Privy Council (at that time the highest court available to Canada) that ruled "... a Lieutenant Governor, when appointed, is as much the representative of Her Majesty for all purposes of provincial government as the Governor General himself is for all purposes of dominion government." Through this ruling, the Crown now affirmed that each province was equal to every other, as well as to Canada. Provinces were now seen as partners in Confederation rather then territories under the rule of Ottawa.

THE KING-BYNG CRISIS, 1926

Liberal Prime Minister Mackenzie King came to office in 1921 with a minority government (one that held the confidence of most of the members of the House of Commons, but could be defeated if all the opposing parties voted against it). In 1925, in an effort to achieve a majority government (50 percent plus 1 of the total seats in the House of Commons), Prime Minister King asked Governor General Lord Byng to dissolve Parliament and call an election. The results of the election were disappointing to the Liberals, who were only able to stay in power with the support of the Conservatives. This minority government was able to stay alive for a few months until a scandal emerged that implicated the Liberal-led government. The Conservative Party (acting as the official opposition) presented a motion that ended in a vote of non-confidence against the government. No longer able to govern, Prime Minister King asked the governor general to dissolve Parliament and call a new election. Noting that they had just had a federal election, and the possible availability of an alternative government in the present Parliament, Lord Byng refused his prime minister's request, inviting Conservative leader Arthur Meighen to form a government. Meighen's government lasted only a short time, falling victim to a motion of non-confidence. Governor General Byng then consented to Meighen's request for dissolution, producing fresh elections and the restoration of Mackenzie King as prime minister. Throughout the campaign the role of the governor general was much criticized, particularly as he was portrayed as an agent of the British government.

THE BALFOUR REPORT, 1926

This report by the British government's Inter-Imperial Relations Committee was a reaction to a push for more autonomy by the self-governing members of the British Empire (led by South Africa). The report recommended that the governor general should strictly represent the Crown as something separate from the British government and therefore only be advised by the prime minister in each dominion.

THE STATUTE OF WESTMINSTER, 1931

This act of the British Parliament was the imperial government's answer to the Balfour Report. The act declared the governments of the dominions (Australia, Newfoundland, the Irish Free State, New Zealand, South Africa, and Canada) equal with, and separate from, that of the United Kingdom. The governor general now represented the Crown rather than the British government. The King's advice concerning the governing of Canada would now come from Canadian ministers rather than from British.

It is important to note that the Canadian government was already operating under the recommendations of the Balfour Report before the Statute of Westminster (1931) was passed. Lord Willingdon had been recommended to King George V as governor general of Canada in 1926 by the Canadian prime minister (after consulting with his British counterpart).

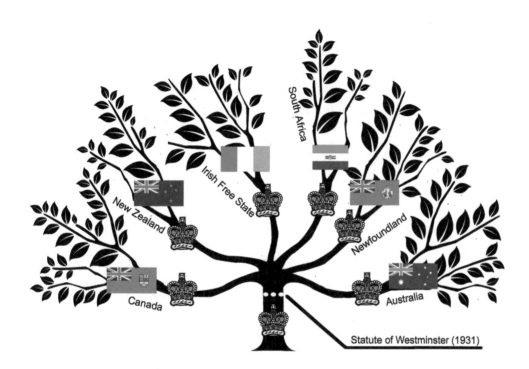

The British Parliament's Statute of Westminster (1931) granted legislative independence (and equality) to the six dominions within the British Empire and Commonwealth at that time: Canada, Australia, the Irish Free State, South Africa, Newfoundland, and New Zealand. This statute made official the emergence of distinct Crowns that already been evolving since the nineteenth century. As shown above, from this point the British Crown evolved into six separate Crowns (it must be noted that the statute was adopted individually, and at separate times, by the dominion governments). Since 1931, many other Crowns have emerged (see Chapter Thirteen). Not every country has allowed their monarchies to grow: Of the dominions represented above, the Irish abolished their Crown in 1936 while South Africa declared itself a republic in 1961. Following a Royal Commission on corruption in its government, the Dominion of Newfoundland suspended its self-government (and distinct Crown) in 1934, reverting back to British rule. Newfoundland (along with Labrador) became a province of Canada in 1949. Image by Nathan Tidridge.

THE CORONATION OF KING GEORGE VI, 1937

During his coronation, George VI was specifically asked if he would govern Canada while respecting its laws. This was the first time that Canada was singled out as a distinct realm by its Sovereign, reaffirming the dramatic changes brought by the Statute of Westminster (1931).

FOREWORD

THIS YEAR FOR THE FIRST TIME IN OUR HISTORY, A reigning monarch of our Empire comes to visit his people in this Dominion beyond the sea, and our neighbours in the United States of America. As King and Queen of Canada, Their Majesties King George VI and Queen Elizabeth will be royally welcomed on their tour and will be given many demonstrations of the love and loyalty of their subjects.

North American Life Assurance Company is proud to participate in this event by presenting "The Visits of Royalty to Canada"— a brief story of other visits made in this country by members of the British Royal Family.

On the occasion of this Royal tour it is opportune to look back on the personalities of those earlier visitors and the customs, manners and events of the days in which they came here. We know that this timely piece of historical study will be greeted with widespread interest. We are most fortunate to have secured the services of C. W. Jefferys, LL.D., well-known Canadian historian and artist, who compiled and wrote the stories and supplied the material from which the drawings were made by A. J. Casson, A.R.C.A.

Those interested in securing additional copies may do so by writing

NORTH AMERICAN LIFE
112 King Street West, Toronto

GEORGE VI   ELIZABETH

OUR PRESENT KING IS THE SECOND SON OF King George V and was born in York Cottage on his father's Sandringham Estate on December 14th, 1895. He was educated at Osborne School in the Isle of Wight, from whence he graduated to Dartmouth Naval Academy. Like his father, King George V, he had a natural inclination toward the sea, and looked forward to a career as a Naval Officer.

In 1912, the Prince joined his first ship, H.M.S. *Cumberland,* and made a cruise to the West Indies in 1913. This was followed by his first visit to our shores, when his ship called at Canada and Newfoundland and he travelled as far inland as Montreal. In September, 1913, as midshipman he joined the *Collingwood,* a battle cruiser.

{3}

ROYAL TOUR OF KING GEORGE VI AND QUEEN ELIZABETH, MAY 17–JUNE 15, 1939

The Royal tour of 1939 was the first time a reigning monarch set foot on Canadian soil. Travelling from Quebec City to Vancouver, and back to Halifax, by train ensured that most Canadians caught a glimpse of the royal couple. Throughout the tour, George VI acted as King of Canada when he granted Royal Assent to eight bills in the Senate, addressed the assembled Parliament, signed a foreign-trade treaty, and received the credentials of the new American ambassador. It was as King of Canada that George VI crossed into the United States on June 7 — Queen Elizabeth II would follow in her father's footsteps by visiting the United States as Queen of Canada in 1957, 1959, and 2010 (the Duke of Cambridge entered the United States officially as a member of the Canadian Royal family in 2011). The Royal tour was the first time Canadians saw their constitutional monarch directly, establishing the tradition of royal tours by the monarch that continue to this day.

THE CANADIAN CITIZENSHIP ACT, 1947

Until this act was proclaimed by King George VI, the residents of Canada were legally British subjects. From January 1, 1947, a common Canadian citizenship was conferred on all the residents of Canada who qualified. The first person to receive their citizenship certificate was Prime Minister Mackenzie King.

LETTERS PATENT CONSTITUTING THE OFFICE OF THE GOVERNOR GENERAL OF CANADA, 1947

Issued by King George VI, these letters instructed the governor general to exercise all powers relating to Canada that previously had been exercised directly by the Sovereign.

From this point on, the governor general could perform all duties of the Sovereign, but always did so in the name of the Sovereign (to emphasize their role as the monarch's representative). Still, for important occasions (example: the Constitution Act, 1982), the Sovereign is often requested by the government to personally attend to them (highlighting their importance to the country).

THE APPOINTMENT OF VINCENT MASSEY AS GOVERNOR GENERAL OF CANADA, 1952

Since the appointment of Vincent Massey to the vice-regal office, every governor general has been a Canadian citizen.

THE ROYAL STYLES AND TITLES ACT, 1953

During the year of her coronation, Queen Elizabeth II became the first monarch to be separately proclaimed as the Canadian monarch by Ottawa. Canada proclaimed that when acting as the Canadian Sovereign, Elizabeth II would be styled:

> Elizabeth the Second, By the Grace of God, of the United Kingdom, Canada, and Her other Realms and Territories Queen, Head of the Commonwealth, Defender of the Faith.

CONSTITUTION ACT, 1982

While Canada was a fully independent country, the government still had to go to the British

Watched by Prime Minister Pierre-Elliot Trudeau, Queen Elizabeth II signs the proclamation of the Canada Act on Parliament Hill, 1982.
Courtesy of Robert Copper and Library and Archives of Canada, e008300499.

Parliament in order to make any changes to its constitution (this had been the decision of earlier Canadian governments because the provinces could not agree on what a formula for altering the constitution should look like). Led by Prime Minister Pierre Elliott Trudeau, intense negotiations on what an amending formula (the procedure that would be used to make any changes to the constitution) would look like began across the country. Finally, in the fall of 1981, nine provincial governments joined with Ottawa in reaching an agreement on cutting the last constitutional tie to the United Kingdom. Quebec refused to sign the pact, although the Supreme Court of Canada ruled that the agreement was legally binding throughout the country.

The resulting document cemented the Crown as part of Canada's constitutional framework — any changes to the institution would require the unanimous consent of Parliament as well as every provincial legislature. The Constitution Act, 1982, also entrenched the Charter of Rights and Freedoms as part of the country's written constitution. Queen

Elizabeth II proclaimed this act on April 17, 1982, transferring the power to amend the constitution from herself as Queen of the United Kingdom to herself as Queen of Canada.

***

PROROGATION OF PARLIAMENT, 2008

Fearing a planned motion of non-confidence, Prime Minister Stephen Harper advised

Governor General Michaëlle Jean to prorogue Parliament on December 4, 2008. The governor general granted the request of her prime minister, but only after lengthy consultation with various constitutional experts. These discussions included consideration of a plan by the opposition parties to form a coalition government. The Queen's representative set two conditions of the dissolution: that Parliament would reconvene soon, and when it did, a budget would have to be successfully passed by the House of Commons. This event awakened many Canadians to the important constitutional role that is played by the governor general and the Sovereign they represent.

Chapter Two

THE CANADIAN CONSTITUTION AND AUTHORITY

Government is a structure that societies put in place in order to regulate the exercise of absolute power. It is the need to control the use of power that has often led to the creation of a constitution. A constitution is the foundation of a country. The statements within it create a concrete image of what a country stands for, how its citizens want it to be run, and how power is to be used. In the United States, the entire framework for the country can be found in one document, but in Canada the same is not true.

Canada has one of the oldest operating constitutions in the world, with roots that include the Magna Carta (signed by King John in 1215), the judgments of St. Louis

The Great Seal of Canada. Since the actual matrix is still used by the Canadian government for official state documents, a rubber impression of the seal is shown at left. Library and Archives of Canada, C-033866.

The Queen views a copy of the Magna Carta during her 2010 visit to Manitoba's Government House.
Department of Canadian Heritage.

of France (around 1260), and the first English Parliament summoned by King Edward I in 1275. Maybe it is because of the vast history involved that our constitution's workings are a mystery to most of Canada's citizens.

The Canadian constitution is a series of written documents and unwritten traditions that have been inherited from the United Kingdom and France as well as any new additions since the Statute of Westminster (1931). The constitution is the result of centuries of evolution. It has roots that stretch back to the very beginnings of English parliaments and French *parlements* and their relationships with their Crowns. The story of our constitution is the long story of the absolute powers of the Sovereign gradually being exercised by representatives of the people. Throughout this process, the Crown has remained as the source of authority, but the right to exercise power is now held within Parliament. Removed from governing directly, the Crown exists to represent the state while protecting the delicate balance of power that has developed in the constitution over the centuries. This balance of

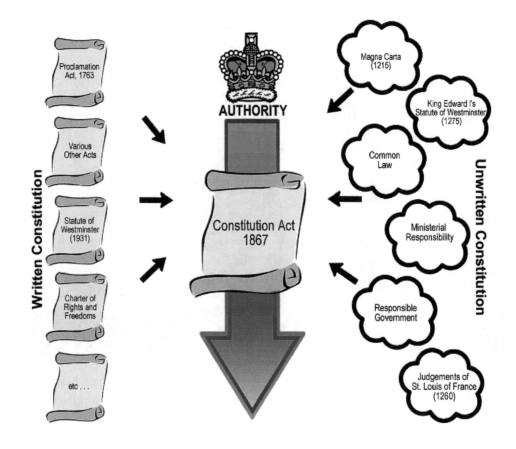

Canada's constitution. The complexity of the constitution is depicted in this chart. The Crown gives the constitution authority as the supreme law of the country.
Created by Nathan Tidridge.

power is reflected in Canada's constitution, which is comprised of two distinct parts: The written constitution and the unwritten constitution.

WRITTEN CONSTITUTION

A string of documents make up Canada's written constitution and include the acts that created some of our various provinces and territories, as well as statutes that spelled out the relationships between Canada's Parliament and that of the United Kingdom. An example of the written constitution would be such documents as the Royal Proclamation (1763), the Statute of Westminster (1931), and the Charter of Rights and Freedoms (1982). All of these documents are seen as the building blocks of Canadian democracy. Taken together, they spell out the boundaries, powers, rights, and responsibilities that make up the Canadian state.

———————

UNWRITTEN CONSTITUTION

The unwritten constitution consists of traditions and conventions that have developed over time, but have never officially been spelled out on paper. These traditions developed slowly as a result of the constantly evolving relationships within Parliament. An example of an unwritten convention that has become integral to our constitution is the practice of responsible government (see Chapter One): that the Sovereign (or their representative) is bound to exercise their power on the advice of elected ministers (called "Cabinet") that command the confidence of the House of Commons. This expectation has been followed by various kings and queens throughout the last two centuries. For the Sovereign not to follow the advice of their elected ministers would be unthinkable unless the government of the day was seriously abusing the power entrusted to them.

The end result is that while formal power is held by the Sovereign, it must be directed by elected ministers. However, the prime minister and his or her Cabinet must be able to command the confidence of the House of Commons (or legislature), meaning they must be able to ensure enough votes in the House to have their bills pass through without being defeated. If a major bill by the government is defeated it is because the ruling party has lost the confidence of the House and power is automatically forfeited back to the Crown. The Sovereign (or governor general, or lieutenant governor) can then call an election, or appoint someone else who can command the confidence of the House (or legislature) to form a government.

———————

CONSTITUTION ACT, 1867, AND THE QUEEN'S PRIVY COUNCIL

At the core of Canada's written and unwritten constitution is the Constitution Act, 1867 (formally called the British North America Act, 1867, and now incorporated into the Constitution Act, 1982). It is within the Constitution Act, 1867, that we find the statement:

> The Executive Government and Authority of and over Canada is declared
> to continue and be vested in the Queen.

This statement places the Crown at the very top of Canada's form of government, highlighting the fact that the authority to hold and use power is ultimately held by the Sovereign. However, in keeping with the practice of responsible government, this power is tempered with the creation of the Queen's Privy Council. The Privy Council exists to advise the Crown on the use of its powers and is made up of:

- Cabinet ministers
- Former Cabinet ministers
- The chief justice of Canada
- Former chief justices
- Former speakers of the House of Commons
- Former speakers of the Senate
- Former governors general
- Distinguished individuals (as a mark of honour)

The main committee (a smaller body within a larger organization) of the Queen's Privy Council is the executive council whose members are always the current members of Cabinet chosen by the prime minister (or provincial premier). Thanks to responsible government, the Crown is bound to follow the advice of the executive council, which is largely made up of elected representatives of the population who command the confidence of the legislature.

To become a Cabinet minister, an individual must make three oaths, highlighting the very structure of our democracy. The first is an oath of allegiance to the Sovereign:

> I, _____, do swear (declare) that I will be faithful and bear true allegiance to Her Majesty Queen Elizabeth the Second, Queen of Canada, Her Heirs and Successors.

The oath of allegiance binds the individual to the Sovereign, who not only represents the state, but each of its citizens. Simply put, representing all Canadians (not a political party, religious belief, or ideology) allows the Queen to be the focal point of loyalty in our system of government.

The second oath is to become a member of the Privy Council (which someone must be before they can be appointed to Cabinet):

> I, _____, do solemnly and sincerely swear (declare) that I shall be a true and faithful servant to Her Majesty Queen Elizabeth the Second, as a member of Her Majesty's Privy Council for Canada. I will in all things to be treated, debated and resolved in Privy Council, faithfully, honestly and truly declare my mind and my opinion. I shall keep secret all matters committed and revealed to me in this capacity, or that shall be secretly treated of in Council. Generally, in all things I shall do as a faithful and true servant ought to do for Her Majesty.
> So help me God.

The oath of a privy councillor is the basis of Cabinet government in Canada. By swearing to keep the secrets revealed to them as privy councillors, members free the prime minister to discuss with them state secrets that should not be made public. This oath, in the name of the Queen, is the foundation of trust that members of the prime minister's (or premier's) Cabinet need in order to conduct the day-to-day business of government. It is why the government members remain united in public while behind closed doors may question the decisions of their leadership.

With the first two oaths as the bedrock, the individual is now ready to take the third oath, which is a simple oath of office:

Mace of the Yukon Legislative Assembly. Presented by Governor General Roland Michener in 1972, the territorial mace was designed by RCMP Corporal Jim Ballantyne. Office of the Speaker of the Northwest Territories Legislative Assembly.

I, _____, do solemnly and sincerely promise and swear (declare) that I will truly and faithfully, and to the best of my skill and knowledge, execute the powers and trusts reposed in me as _____.
So help me God.

It is because of the important relationships established with the above oaths, as well as the practice of responsible government that the phrases *Governor General in Council* or *Lieutenant Governor in Council* (in Nova Scotia, the phrase *Governor in Council*) are used — emphasizing that Canada is a *constitutional* monarchy.

Showing Canada's unwritten belief in responsible government, orders-in-council (documents issued by the Queen's representatives that direct certain actions to be taken based on existing laws) read:

Federally:
His Excellency the Governor General in Council, on the recommendation of the [Member of Cabinet] …

Provincially (all provinces use this phrasing except Quebec, Nova Scotia, and Ontario):
The Lieutenant Governor in Council …

AUTHORITY

All of the above centres on the Crown as the source of formal authority for Canada's government. In other words, it is from the Crown that our institutions officially receive their legitimacy. This is represented by the Royal Arms of Canada (see Chapter Three). The Crown is depicted above the arms in a relationship that highlights its role as the source of formal authority for the country.

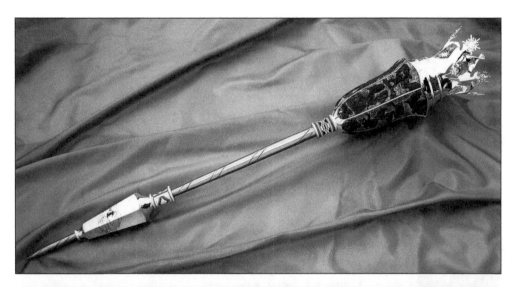

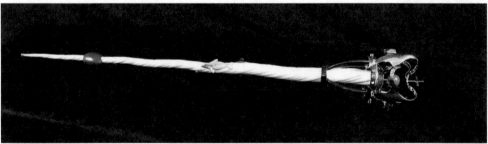

Top: Mace of the Northwest Territories Legislative Assembly. The NWT had its first mace presented to it in 1956, but to mark the separation of Nunavut in 1999, a new mace was ordered. Designed by Bill Nasogaluak, Dolphus Cadieux, and Allyson M. Simmie, the new mace (unveiled in 2000) is one of the most unique in the Commonwealth. What sets it apart is its sound — within the shaft and foot of the mace are thirty-three pebbles, one from every community in the territory. When the mace is moved, an effect like that of a rainstick is created — representing the united voice of the people. Office of the Speaker of the Yukon Legislative Assembly.

Bottom: Mace of the Nunavut Legislative Assembly. Unveiled in 1999, the territorial mace is made out of a narwhal tusk with a crown formed by common loons. A two-and-a-quarter carat diamond from western Nunavut is mounted on the mace's tip. A team of Nunavut artists (Mariano Aupilardjuk, Inuk Charlie, Paul Malliki, Mathew Nunqingaq, Simata Pitsiulak, and Joseph Suqslaq) worked on the design. Office of the Speaker of the Nunavut Legislative Assembly.

© HOC-CDC

SENATE   SÉNAT

CANADA

Above: Badge of the Senate of Canada. Created by the Canadian Heraldic Authority in 2008, the badge depicts the mace used in the Senate. Office of the Speaker of the Senate of Canada.

Left: Badge of the House of Commons. Created by the Canadian Heraldic Authority in 2008, the badge depicts the mace used in the House of Commons —a replacement of the 1916 mace that was lost in the great fire that destroyed the original Parliament Buildings. ©House of Commons.

PARLIAMENT

The Constitution Act, 1867, established a Parliament for Canada made up of three parts : the Queen, the Senate, and the House of Commons. Within Parliament are exercised two of the three powers of government: the executive and the legislative (the judiciary is exercised through the Supreme Court of Canada).

The executive branch of government is comprised of those who ultimately exercise power: the Sovereign (or her representative) and her advisors (members of the Queen's Privy Council and its main committee, the Cabinet). The Crown's advisors (or ministers) must be drawn from the legislative branch of government, and largely from the elected House of Commons (following responsible government). Together, the House of Commons and the Senate exercise the legislative power of government (it is through them that bills are presented and debated before the Sovereign — or her representative — enter the Senate to give their final approval to make it a law — this final act of approval is called Royal Assent).

To separate the Sovereign from Parliament is impossible. James Jerome, Speaker of the House of Commons from 1974–1979, explained that to remove the monarchy from Parliament would be like taking the nucleus out of an atom:

> Can we possibly conceive of any process by which some elected Canadian official, whom we might call a President instead of a Governor General, might be entrusted by us with all the power and authority we know repose in the Monarch?
>
> The answer of course is that any such hybrid is most unlikely. It would be all but impossible to graft such a feature onto our Parliamentary system. If it were to be attempted, it would mean a total constitutional overhaul ...

Mr. Jerome went on to explain:

> ... Parliament has endured because it works, particularly in terms of control. The Queen, who appears to have supreme authority, must act upon the advice of her prime minister. The prime minister, who also appears to have supreme authority, acquires that status only by commanding support of a majority of the members of the House of Commons. Within the House of Commons, responsibility for directing the scrutiny of the actions of the government falls to the leader of the majority opposition party, who fulfills that function as a direct responsibility to the Monarch in the official capacity of Leader of Her Majesty's Loyal Opposition.

Canada's Parliament. Reading the 1957 Speech from the Throne, Queen Elizabeth II said to the assembled senators and members of parliament, "I greet you as your Queen. Together we constitute the Parliament of Canada." Image by Nathan Tidridge.

PROVINCIAL GOVERNMENT

It is also within the Constitution Act, 1867, that the four original provincial legislatures were created making Canada a federal state (a state in which the authority to make laws is divided between national and provincial governments). The legislatures were given control over specific areas (municipalities, marriage, and education), which were typically local, while the federal Parliament would handle things such as the military, spending power, and maintaining peace, order, and good government. Provincial parliaments are called legislative assemblies, except for Newfoundland and Labrador, which has a House of Assembly and Quebec, which has a National Assembly.

To represent the Crown, provinces have appointed to them by the governor general-in-council a lieutenant governor who, along with the Legislative Assembly, makes up the two parts of a provincial legislature (some legislatures originally included a legislative council,

The Honourable Mayann E. Francis, lieutenant governor of Nova Scotia, swears in her new premier, Darrell Dexter, in 2009. Office of the Lieutenant Governor of Nova Scotia.

but today no province has an upper chamber). The lieutenant governor is the personal representative of the Sovereign in their province — emphasizing that Canada's national Crown is comprised of ten provincial Crowns that are distinct from each another. The Honourable Hilary Weston (lieutenant governor of Ontario, 1997–2002) explains:

> Rather, like the governor general, we take our constitutional advice from the premier and his or her ministers, and we are the legal personification of jurisdictions such as education, in which the provinces are autonomous and Sovereign.

In other words, the provincial Crown exists to safeguard the independence of each province, thus protecting the areas entrusted to their governments by the constitution.

RESERVE POWERS OF THE CROWN: THE ROYAL PREROGATIVE

The power a federal or provincial government has is only temporary, and must be returned to the Crown when it no longer has the confidence of the House of Commons or legislature. This means that while governments come and go, the institution of the Crown remains as a fixed point in our democracy federally and provincially.

In extreme cases, such as when a prime minister/premier and Cabinet are abusing their powers, the Sovereign (or her representative) could refuse to follow their minister's advice, removing their authority to govern. As the source of authority, the institution of the Crown gives Canadians a way in which to dissolve a parliament, or defeat a government that is violating the constitution. The Queen (or her representatives) has the power to refuse Royal Assent (the final stage of a bill to becoming a law), or even to dismiss a prime minister. Professor Frank McKinnon explained these powers as the Crown acting as a "constitutional fire extinguisher."

A fire extinguisher exists to be used in extreme emergencies — not on a day-to-day basis. It is bright and colourful, so people always know that it is there if needed. The Crown works

One of the Queen's Royal Prerogatives is the power to declare war on other sovereign states. However, the unwritten constitution and the idea of responsible government dictate that the Queen can only exercise this prerogative on the advice of her ministers. Reproduced here is the instrument sent by Prime Minister William Lyon Mackenzie King formally advising King George VI to declare war on Germany in 1939. The King's signature signals his approval.

Library and Archives of Canaada, R219-100-6-E.

Approved

George R.I

OFFICE OF THE PRIME MINISTER
CANADA

The Prime Minister of Canada presents his humble duty to His Majesty the King.

It is expedient that a Proclamation should be issued in the name of His Majesty, in Canada, declaring that a state of war with the German Reich has existed in Canada as and from September tenth.

The Prime Minister of Canada, accordingly, humbly submits to His Majesty the petition of The King's Privy Council for Canada that His Majesty may approve the issuing of such a Proclamation in His name.

The Prime Minister of Canada remains His Majesty's most faithful and obedient servant.

Prime Minister of Canada.

Ottawa, September 10th, 1939.

this way. Elaborate ceremonies exist to highlight the constitutional role of the Crown, but seldom involve actually using them. A fire extinguisher exists to put a stop to any fires that get out of control, but it is something people never hope they will have to use. The fact that the extinguisher exists makes those people living around it feel safer. Use of the Crown's powers are rare, but they exist to ensure that things in government don't get too far out of hand.

Called "reserve powers" or the "royal prerogative," the Sovereign (or her representative) still acts independently on certain occasions: the appointment of a prime minister, accepting or refusing a request to dissolve a parliament or legislature, and forcing an election. However, even the reserve powers have developed unwritten traditions which are usually never broken.

In the case of the appointment of a prime minister (one of the duties of the Crown is to ensure that the country always has a prime minister), the Sovereign traditionally appoints the leader of the party that holds the most seats in the House of Commons (meaning that they are able to command the confidence of the House). In an age of coalition governments and close election results, the choice of a prime minister can become less obvious. It is such cases that require the institution of the Crown to exist so that there is a way to ensure that the country always has a clear leader of the government.

―――――――

ROYAL ASSENT

In order for a bill to become law in Parliament (or one of the provincial legislatures), Royal Assent must be granted. This is the last step in a long journey through Parliament (or a legislature) that grants authority to the new law in the name of the Sovereign. Ceremonies conferring Royal Assent (signalled by a nod from the Sovereign, or her representative) vary throughout the country, but all convey a very powerful message. By giving Royal Assent to a law passed by the government of the day, the Crown (as guardian of the constitution) represents the people agreeing to live under the rule of law. Since the Queen embodies the state and its citizens, the act of Royal Assent emphasizes that we all must live equally under the law.

This example from Ontario (June 17, 2004) highlights the important relationship between the Crown and its elected representatives:

- 9:35 p.m.: His Honour the Lieutenant Governor of the Province entered the chamber of the Legislative Assembly and took his seat upon the Throne.
- The Speaker addressed His Honour as follows:
  "May it please Your Honour:
  The Legislative Assembly of the Province has, at its present meetings thereof, passed certain bills to which, in the name and on behalf of the said Legislative Assembly, I respectfully request Your Honour's assent."
- The Deputy Clerk and Executive Director of Legislative Services then read the titles of the bills that had passed …
- To these Acts the Royal Assent was announced by the Clerk of the Legislative Assembly in the following words:
  "In Her Majesty's name, His Honour the Lieutenant Governor doth assent to these bills."

Can the Crown refuse assent? Former private secretary to the lieutenant governor of Prince Edward Island, James W. Macnutt, wrote that the theory behind refusing assent is sound, however it has not been practised in decades (the last representative of the Crown to refuse Royal Assent was by the lieutenant governor of Prince Edward Island in 1935). When a prerogative is not exercised for a prolonged period of time, a perception is created that it is no longer relevant, which over time turns into fact. That is why our constitution is largely unwritten so such a process can be allowed to continue. Today, if a governor general or lieutenant governor refused assent to a bill that had been passed through an elected legislature (and did not violate the constitution) there would be a huge outcry by the general public, which would probably end with the removal of the vice-regal representative from office. Still, the process of Royal Assent exists to safeguard against elected legislatures that could — in extreme cases — violate our constitutional rules and traditions (while not in common practice, it is important that the mechanism to control elected officials still exists), as well as remind the government that it is the people that finally must agree to live under the rule of law in order for it to work.

Reading the final acts of Parliament and the legislatures again underscores how Canada's parliamentary democracy works. The federal act that created the new territory of Nunavut (The Nunavut Act, 1993) reads:

> *Her Majesty, by and with the advice and consent of the Senate and House of Commons of Canada, enacts as follows …*

Provincially, the act that created the National Assembly of Quebec (Act Respecting the National Assembly, 1983) states:

> *Her Majesty, by and with the advice and consent of the National Assembly of Québec, enacts as follows…*

In having both a written and unwritten constitution, Canada's parliamentary democracy avoids "painting itself into a corner" by having rules that cannot adapt to changing times. This growth is a fine balance between the executive and legislative branches of government, as well as the federal and provincial parliaments. What is common throughout this evolution is the institution of the Crown as the ultimate source of authority and fixed point in our democracy.

Chapter Three

THE QUEEN OF CANADA

The Canadian Oath of Citizenship:
I swear (or affirm)
That I will be faithful
And bear true allegiance
To Her Majesty Queen Elizabeth the Second
Queen of Canada
Her Heirs and Successors
And that I will faithfully observe
The laws of Canada
And fulfill my duties as a Canadian citizen.

PERSONIFYING THE STATE

The Honourable Myron Kowalsky, Speaker of the Legislative Assembly of Saskatchewan, explained during a visit to the province by Prince Charles that the power of our oath of allegiance is that it is not to a constitution or flag, but rather "to the person of the Sovereign."

Individuals become citizens in direct relationship with the Sovereign, not a commitment to a particular revolution, racial or ethnic group, or the ideals of a governing party.

Queen Elizabeth II personifies the state, which means that she is the human face of our complex form of government. More than just a Head of State, the Queen represents the thousands of rules, regulations, and centuries of traditions that make up our Canadian democracy. The Queen also represents all Canadians in a way that a flag, politician, or ideal (all of which can be easily changed) cannot. Kevin MacLeod, Usher of the Black Rod and Canadian Secretary to the Queen, explains: "It is a remarkably simple yet powerful principle: Canada is personified by the Sovereign just as the Sovereign is personified by Canada."

The heraldic symbol used by the Canadian government — the coat of arms — is actually the Queen's Arms in Right of Canada. They are her own arms, representing her as the human face of the state. It is for these reasons that things like government letterhead display the arms, showing that the messages come from agents of "Her Majesty's Government." The same goes provincially. The arms of each province are the Queen's since she is the personification of their autonomy within Confederation.

When we honour the Crown, we are celebrating the very best of Canada. Similarly, when we are honoured by the Crown we are being celebrated by the whole country.

The Queen speaks at a state dinner held at the Fairmont Royal York Hotel in Toronto, 2010. Department of Canadian Heritage.

Removed from government, the Crown has been called "the ship of state," while the government of the day is merely in control of the steering wheel. Another way to understand this relationship is by looking at government as if it is a car:

- The car is in the name of the Queen. It is her name that is on the ownership. The governor general represents the Queen when she is out of the country.

*The Queen's Arms
in Right of Canada.
Reproduced with the permission
of the Government of Canada.*

- The Queen is not able to drive the car herself, and must select a driver (the prime minister) who is able to maintain the confidence of everyone else travelling in the vehicle. It is the prime minister who ultimately decides which trip to take (which policies and laws he/she wants the government to pursue).
- Helping the driver are the passengers (the Cabinet and other Members of Parliament, including the opposition) who help decide which directions, and which roads, the car will take to reach its final destination (which bills will they introduce into law, and how will they be constructed and/ or critiqued). If the driver and passengers take the car down a dangerous or unconstitutional road, the Queen embodies the institution that can remove them.
- Before leaving, the Senate always checks over the directions to make sure there aren't any errors, and that the path that has been chosen is the best one for the car to take. If the Senate has any concerns they can return the directions with their own recommendations for improvement or reject them all together.

The Queen's Arms in Right of Saskatchewan. Reproduced with the permission of the Government of Saskatchewan.

THE SEPARATION OF THE HEAD OF GOVERNMENT FROM THE STATE

The separation of the government from the state is an important one, and something that does not exist in countries like the United States. The prime minister, as head of government, is permitted to use the machinery of the state (represented by the Crown) as long as they maintain the confidence of the House of Commons. This distinction is important — the prime minister "uses" the machinery of state, but does not possess it. All of

The Queen's Personal Canadian Flag flies over the HMCS St. John's (signalling that the Queen is aboard) during the 2010 International Fleet Review in Halifax. This flag was approved by the Queen in 1961. Department of Canadian Heritage.

the prime minister's power is borrowed, which reminds them that it can be removed. Acts are proclaimed in the name of the Sovereign, not the sitting prime minister, to underline this relationship and keep egos in check. During the opening of Parliament, the Queen (or her representative) sits in the throne because they embody the state. The prime minister sits in a chair to the right of the throne (the leader of the opposition sits to the left), visibly lower to remind the head of government of their place in our democracy. As the personification of the state and its people, no one is higher than the Sovereign.

The most important part of the opening of Parliament is the reading of the Speech from the Throne. This speech, written by the prime minister, outlines the direction and policies that the government will pursue during the next session of Parliament. The representative of the Crown

Queen Elizabeth II reads the Speech from the Throne in Ottawa, 1957. On the Queen's right is John G. Diefenbaker, prime minister of Canada.
National Film Board of Canada / Library and Archives of Canada, PA-111420.

reads this speech as the personified state, detailing the direction its government is planning to take. During the Nova Scotian Speech from the Throne, this relationship is emphasized by the fact that the lieutenant governor refers to the government as "*my* government."

As Queen of Canada, Elizabeth II has been at the focus of tremendous developments in Canada's evolution as a country (this makes sense, since she has reigned over the country for 41 percent of its history since Confederation!). Some notable events include:

- Opening Canadian Parliament (1957 and 1977)
- Opening the St. Lawrence Seaway (1959)
- Approving a personal standard to represent her as Queen of Canada (1961)
- Proclaiming the national maple leaf flag (1965)
- Celebrating the one hundredth anniversary of Confederation (1967)
- Creating the Order of Canada (1967)
- Celebrating the one hundredth anniversary of the Northwest Territories and Manitoba's entry into Confederation (1970)
- Celebrating the one hundredth anniversary of British Columbia's entry into Confederation (1971)
- Opening the Montreal Summer Olympic Games (1976)
- Opening the XI Commonwealth Games in Edmonton, Alberta (1978)
- Approving the creation of a distinctly Canadian standard for the governor general (1981)
- Proclaiming the Constitution Act, 1982
- Celebrating the 125th anniversary of Confederation (1992)
- Approving the creation of the Canadian Victoria Cross (1993)
- Celebrating the five hundredth anniversary of the landing of Giovanni Caboto (John Cabot) in Newfoundland (1997)
- Celebrating the one hundredth anniversaries of both Alberta and Saskatchewan (2005)
- Commemorating the ninetieth anniversary of the Battle of Vimy Ridge (2007)
- Commemorating the centennial of the Royal Canadian Navy (2010)
- Unveiling the cornerstone for the Canadian Museum for Human Rights (2010)

———

THE IMPORTANCE OF CEREMONY

The presence of the Queen at the events brings something that is very hard to describe, and for politicians to mimic. There is a quality about the Crown that carries with it the weight of centuries of history and respect. Jacques Monet, respected historian and author, explains:

> As a symbol, the Crown speaks to the imagination and the emotions. It appeals to the senses through ceremonies which vary extensively according to circumstance and place, but which always include some rite or symbolic act which will lift the moment out of the ordinary.

It is this idea of "out of the ordinary" that the Queen of Canada lends to significant events in Canada's life; moments where the citizens can stand back together to pause and reflect on what is happening in front of them. The importance of such ceremonies in the life of a country is incalculable, for it is through these events that the stories and messages of what that society stands for are acted out. Every society attaches a great importance on ceremony that goes far beyond the need to entertain tourists or add a splash of colour to a particular event. For an example of such a ceremony, Canada needs only to look at the opening of Parliament to realize why acting out our traditions is so important.

THE OPENING OF PARLIAMENT

The ancient ceremony of the opening of Canada's Parliament was inherited from the United Kingdom, and contains within it lessons that are acted out in order to explain how our democracy has evolved. The opening begins with the Sovereign (or the governor general) seated in the throne in the Senate. Surrounding the throne are the senators, diplomats, and other dignitaries in formal dress for the most important event of the Canadian state. In front of the throne are the justices of the Supreme Court.

Directed by the Speaker of the Senate, the Usher of the Black Rod exits the Senate and makes their way to the House of Commons. As the messenger of the Sovereign, Black Rod stops in front of the Commons, the doors to which have been shut. The doors are shut to highlight the independence of the House of Commons from the Crown and Senate — an act of defiance that reminds us of the truly independent nature of the Lower House of Parliament. Within the House of Commons, Members of Parliament are free to express themselves, enjoying parliamentary privileges that the Crown cannot abuse. In fact, the Queen or her representatives cannot enter the House of Commons. This is so that the Members can be assured the freedom of expression. Played out every time Parliament is opened, this important lesson of the independence of the Commons is one of the keys to understanding Canada's democracy.

Using an ebony rod, Black Rod knocks three times before they are admitted into the House of Commons to inform its members that the monarch (or governor general) desires them to come to the Senate. After the Usher of the Black Rod departs, the Speaker leads the procession to the Senate. Behind the Speaker is the sergeant-at-arms with the Commons' mace (their symbol of royal authority) and clerks, followed by the Members of Parliament. The members talk and joke as they head to the Senate — reminding everyone that it is the elected representatives that exercise true power in Parliament.

Once the Members enter the Senate chamber, Canada's Parliament is fully assembled: Queen, Senate, and Commons. In that one moment everyone is in their constitutional place — all the actors of our state on stage together. Like hitting a reset button, everyone is physically reminded how everything fits together in our system of government. The state and its people are embodied by the Crown, and the government by the officials assembled around it.

In his book *Building for Democracy*, James W. Macnutt explores the basic designs of the legislatures of Nova Scotia, Prince Edward Island, and New Brunswick, and how they were constructed to reflect maritime concepts of democracy. Highlighting the importance of ceremony in the provinces, Macnutt writes about the moment the lieutenant governor reads the Speech from the Throne:

> The constitutional role of each element is reflected in the relative positions
> of superiority and deference of the parties. The Lieutenant-Governor, as

the monarch's representative, is head of the legislature and its elected members and an essential (not just ceremonial) part of government, with an actual function in the development of the legislature.

————————

THE CANADIAN CROWN AS A COMPOUND MONARCHY — THE QUEEN AND HER TEAM OF GOVERNORS

Canada has the unique situation in that the Queen is shared by fifteen other countries across the globe and that Her Majesty does not live in Canadian territory. The modern Crown is a product of the peaceful dismantling of the British Empire and the reinvention of the monarchy as the embodiment of sixteen independent countries. While the person of the Queen remains the same, the institution she embodies has become as varied as the realms that recognize her as their Queen. The Crown's ability to evolve reflects its strength as an institution, and for Canada this evolution has involved the creation of what Dr. David Smith calls a "Compound Monarchy."

Canada's Compound Monarchy. Image by Nathan Tidridge.

In Canada, the monarch is represented at the national level by the governor general. Representing the Queen at the provincial level are the lieutenant governors. Territories do not have Sovereignty over their own jurisdictions separately from the federal government so they do not have a direct representative of the Crown. This "team of governors" (a term coined by Frank MacKinnon) joins an ancient and global monarchy with local representatives that keep it grounded in this country. Dr. D. Michael Jackson, C.V.O., explains in *The Canadian Monarchy in Saskatchewan*:

> ... the Canadian Crown benefits from the mystique and historic prestige of an ancient

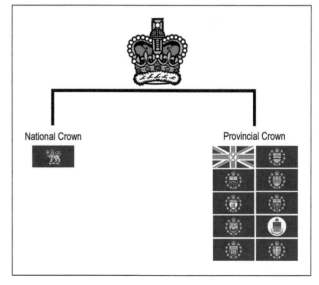

National Crown

Provincial Crown

hereditary monarchy, while making it thoroughly indigenous through the local representatives of the Sovereign. One cannot do without the other: the Governor General and Lieutenant Governors derive their legitimacy and prestige from the Queen ... [and] the Queen is truly Canadian by virtue of her vice-regal representatives.

While it is the Queen who remains the focus in our system of government, the team of governors surrounding her ensures that the institution remains tied to the local community.

Chapter Four

THE GOVERNOR GENERAL AND THE NATIONAL CROWN

There are always those who question the need for our country's ties with the Crown. But I am reminded of the words of Robertson Davies, who said: "The Crown is the abiding and unshakeable element in government, politicians may come and go, but the Crown remains … [it] is the consecrated spirit of Canada." The monarchy will always have a role in our society because it is part of our history. The Crown helps to define who we are, where we came from and where we are going.

— The Right Honourable Dr. David Johnston, 28th Governor General since Confederation, during the unveiling of an image of Queen Elizabeth II in the Senate foyer. December, 2010.

For many Canadians, their first encounter with the Canadian Crown is the Queen's representative, the governor general. Appointed by the Queen on the advice of the Canadian prime minister, the governor general exercises the powers of the Crown in the name of the Sovereign. Sometimes referred to as the vice-regal representative, the governor general serves at the pleasure of the Queen. This means that their time in office is not a fixed term, although it traditionally lasts between five and seven years.

An engraving of Michel Particelli, a much-hated courtier who rose to become a superintendent of finance in the courts of Louis XIII and XIV. This portrait is often misidentified as Samuel de Champlain, as no true images of Champlain are known to exist. Library and Archives of Canada, Copy negative C-006643.

The office of Queen's representative claims a history that stretches back to Samuel de Champlain, who acted in the name of the French Crown from 1627 to 1635. From Champlain to the present-day governor general, the institution's history stretches back over four hundred years, making it the oldest Canadian public office. Since 1952 the governor general has always been a Canadian (although the first Canadian-born individual to serve in the office was Pierre de Vaudreuil from 1755 to 1760).

Ever since King George VI signed the *Letters Patent Constituting the Office of the Governor General* in 1947, the governor general has been authorized to exercise most of the prerogatives and constitutional responsibilities of the Sovereign in Canada. These responsibilities include:

- serving as commander-in-chief of the Canadian Forces
- ensuring the country always has a prime minister
- summoning, proroguing, and dissolving Parliament
- delivering the Speech from the Throne
- granting Royal Assent to legislation
- representing Canada overseas
- hosting visiting dignitaries
- receiving foreign high commissioners and ambassadors (since 1977, governors general have signed the letters of credence of Canadian high commissioners and ambassadors, giving them the authority to represent the government).
- honouring Canadians
- granting armorial bearings

In a personal letter to Governor General Vincent Massey (1952–1959), the Queen wrote that the most important function of the vice-regal representative is to maintain a "right relationship between the Crown and the people of Canada." This relationship is the

Governor General Michaëlle Jean meets United States President Barack Obama during his visit to Canada in 2008 (the first international visit of his presidency).
©Her Majesty The Queen in Right of Canada represented by the Office of the Secretary to the Governor General (2009). Sgt. Serge Gouin, Rideau Hall. Reproduced with permission of the Office of the Secretary to the Governor General.

source of the office's legitimacy and authority. The Crown goes far beyond being simply a "rubber stamp," as Senator Serge Joyal reminded Canadians in 2010:

> The Crown represents everything that is stable in our society, and as the representative of the Crown in Canada, the governor general has an obligation to make sure that the respected institutions continue to be meaningful.

Governor General Jules Léger (1974–1979) stated during his term that, "If I had to define the constitutional responsibilities of the governor general in a few words, I would say that he provides a pause for reflection." The institution of the Crown affords pauses in government which give Canadians a chance to take stock of what is going on politically, reflecting on legislation before it becomes concrete law.

THE RIGHTS OF THE CROWN

Along with the constitutional responsibilities exercised by the Queen's representative are the inherited "rights" that a modern constitutional monarch has in relation to the government (as articulated by Walter Bagehot):

The right to …

- be consulted
- encourage
- warn

Although Bagehot wrote about these rights in 1867, representatives of the Crown (both the governor general and the lieutenant governors) claim them as important parts of their job. In fact, Governor General David Johnston alluded to the importance of Bagehot's rights during a CBC interview shortly after his appointment in 2010. "One hopes," Dr. Johnston stated, "there's an exchange of views and advice between the Queen's representative, as being objective and removed from politics, and those who are elected to practice politics …"

COMMANDER-IN-CHIEF

The Constitution Act, 1867 (Section 15), declares the Queen to be commander-in-chief of the land and naval militia (now called the Canadian Forces), a role exercised by the governor general since 1947. Over the centuries, there has always been a strong relationship between the Crown and the military that continues today.

The governor general actively visits Canadian Forces personnel and their families, attends military events and presentations, and awards military honours to Canada's soldiers. Some governors general have worn a military uniform at various events in their

Governor General David Johnston presents the 1st Battalion of The Royal Canadian Regiment Battle Group with the Commander-in-Chief Unit Commendation (which comprises of a pendant, scroll, and insignia) during a visit to Afghanistan in 2010. The commendation is given to a unit that has performed an extraordinary deed or activity of a rare high standard in extremely hazardous circumstances during wartime or warlike instances. ©Her Majesty The Queen in Right of Canada represented by the Office of the Secretary to the Governor General (2010). Sgt. Serge Gouin, Rideau Hall. Reproduced with permission of the Office of the Secretary to the Governor General.

capacities as commander-in-chief (a specially designed flag/general officer's uniform). To date, Vincent Massey, Georges Vanier, Roland Michener, Edward Schreyer, Jeanne Sauvé, Ramon Hnatyshyn, and Michaëlle Jean have all worn uniforms in their roles as head of Canada's military forces.

As well as being commander-in-chief, the governor general also holds honorary positions in the Canadian Forces as regimental colonel for:

- The Governor General's Foot Guards
- The Governor General's Horse Guards
- The Canadian Grenadier Guards

Badge of the Governor General's Horse Guards. This is the most senior militia regiment in Canada, and one of the three household regiments in the Primary Reserve of the Canadian Armed Forces (the other two being the Governor General's Horse Guards and the Canadian Grenadier Guards). National Defence. Reproduced with the permission of the Minister of Public Works and Government Services, 2010.

HONOURING CANADIANS

Over the years, governors general have created awards to highlight various aspects of Canadian society, using the prestige of the Crown to celebrate the accomplishments of its citizens. The awards offered in the name of the governor general include (the quotations are taken from the official descriptions provided by Rideau Hall):

The Governor General's Academic Medal

Instituted by Lord Dufferin in 1873; students across the country encounter the bronze academic medal at their high school graduation ceremonies. The bronze medal is awarded to students with the highest overall average in their graduating year (including their grades 11 and 12 marks). The medal also exists in collegiate bronze (college), silver (university undergraduate), and gold (university graduate).

Governor General's Literary Awards

Lord Tweedsmuir devised this award in 1937 as a way of recognizing the literary talents of Canadians. Every year awards are given to books (both English and French language) in the categories of Fiction, Non-fiction, Poetry, Drama, Children's Literature (text), Children's Literature (illustration), and Translation (from French to English, and from English to French).

Governor General's Performing Arts Awards

This lifetime award was created by Ramon John Hnatyshyn in 1992 to honour a lifetime of contribution to the cultural life of the country.

Governor General's Medals in Architecture

These medals grew out of the Massey Medals created in the 1950s, recognizing and celebrating outstanding design in projects created by Canadian architects.

Michener Award

Founded by Roland Michener in 1970, this award highlights the impact of the news media on the country. The recipients are chosen annually "on the basis of hard-hitting impact, journalistic professionalism and what resources were available for the project."

Governor General's Awards in Commemoration of the Persons Case

Created on the fiftieth anniversary (1979) of the decision by the Judicial Committee of the British Privy Council that Canadian women were "persons," this award salutes "contributions to the advancement of women's equality and celebrate Canada's evolution as an inclusive society."

The Governor General's Caring Canadian Award

Created by Roméo LeBlanc in 1996, this award celebrates voluntarism and "the fine example set by these special volunteers whose compassion and charitableness are such a part of the Canadian character."

Governor General's Awards for Excellence in Teaching Canadian History

Also created in 1996, this award, conceived by Canada's National History Society, recognizes excellence in the teaching of Canadian history.

Governor General's International Award for Canadian Studies

Established in 1995 by the International Council for Canadian

Lapel pin worn by recipients of the Caring Canadian Award. © Her Majesty The Queen in Right of Canada represented by the Office of the Secretary to the Governor General (2004). Cpl Hago Vanayan, DND. Reproduced with permission of the Office of the Secretary to the Governor General.

The Governor General's Northern Medal. © Her Majesty The Queen in Right of Canada represented by the Office of the Secretary to the Governor General (2005). MCpl Paz Quilllé, Rideau Hall. Reproduced with permission of the Office of the Secretary to the Governor General.

Studies with the support of Ramon John Hnatyshyn. This award celebrates living scholars who have made an outstanding contribution to the field of Canadian studies internationally.

Governor General's Awards in Visual and Media Arts

Also founded under Roméo LeBlanc, these awards "recognize a stellar array of artists and arts volunteers for their outstanding lifetime contributions to Canada's cultural life."

The Governor General's Northern Medal

Adrienne Clarkson created this medal in 2005 to recognize individuals "whose actions and achievements have contributed to the evolution and constant reaffirmation of the Canadian North as part of our national identity."

The Governor General's Award in Celebration of the Nation's Table

Founded by Michaëlle Jean in 2010, this culinary award "celebrates the outstanding efforts of Canadians in improving the quality, variety and sustainability of all elements and ingredients of our nation's table."

FOSTERING CANADIAN CULTURE

Governors General the Marquess of Dufferin (1873–1878) and Marquess of Lorne (1878–1883) are credited with promoting the idea of Canadian national art. Governor General Dufferin patronized centralized cultural institutions such as the Ontario Society of Artists and used his influence to preserve the architectural heritage of Quebec. The Marquess of Lorne went on to found the Royal Canadian Academy, leading to the establishment of the National Gallery of Canada in 1882 (author and historian Jonathan Vance quotes Lorne in *A History of Canadian Culture* as saying that the National Gallery came into being after "… a marvelous amount of bitterness and bad language; half the artists are ready just now to choke the other half with their paint brushes").

Lapel pin of the Governor General's Award in Celebration of the Nation's Table. ©Her Majesty The Queen in Right of Canada represented by the Office of the Secretary to the Governor General (2010). Sgt. Serge Gouin, Rideau Hall. Reproduced with permission of the Office of the Secretary to the Governor General.

A champion of Canadian culture, the Marquess of Lorne also founded the Royal Society of Canada with a mandate to "… promote learning and intellectual accomplishments of exceptional quality. The Society recognizes remarkable contributions in the arts, humanities and sciences, as well as in Canadian public life." Lorne is also credited with trying to establish a museum dedicated to Sir John A. Macdonald (something that has yet to materialize), advocated for the creation of a federal ministry of culture, and even commissioned Sir Arthur Sullivan to write the music for a poem he had written entitled "Dominion Hymn" in the hopes that it would become the national anthem. The idea of two Englishmen penning the national anthem upset the St. Jean Baptiste Society of Quebec and it quickly died. The lieutenant governor of Quebec (the Honourable Théodore Robitaille) later asked Calixa Lavallée and Judge Adolphe-Basile Routhier to compose an anthem, the end result being "O Canada."

While there are numerous other examples of the vice-regal influence in the development and protection of Canadian culture, Vincent Massey stands out as a giant in this field. It was the Royal Commission on National Development in the Arts, Letters, and Sciences (nicknamed

Left: His Excellency, the Right Honourable David Johnston, governor general of Canada since his installation on October 1, 2010. ©Her Majesty The Queen in Right of Canada represented by the Office of the Secretary to the Governor General (2010). Sgt. Serge Gouin, Rideau Hall. Reproduced with permission of the Office of the Secretary to the Governor General.

Right: Lord Stanley of Preston, governor general of Canada (1888–93). The earliest known hockey game played at Buckingham Palace was organized by Lord Stanley's five sons on a frozen pond out on the grounds. The opposing team, made up of palace officials, included the future King Edward VII and King George V. Library and Archives of Canada, R12631-1.

the "Massey Commission"), published one year before its namesake and commissioner would be appointed to the office of Queen's representative in 1952, that sounded an alarm about the poor state of Canadian culture. One section of the report commented that Grade 8 students knew more about the fourth of July (American Independence Day) than the significance of July 1st! The 146 recommendations (including one to create a national order — see Chapter Nine) by this commission created awareness, triggering a renewed effort to foster and protect Canadian art, literature, and other important aspects of the country's culture.

―――――――

PATRON SCOUT OF CANADA

The governor general is also the Patron Scout of Canada, honorary head of the Canadian branch of the international scouting movement (encompassing Beaver Scouts, Cub Scouts, Scouts, Venturer Scouts, and Rover Scouts) that was founded in 1908 by Lieutenant General Robert Stephenson Smyth Baden-Powell and later granted a Royal Charter by King George V in 1912. It was Baden-Powell who asked Governor General Earl Grey in 1910 to organize scouting in Canada.

Called the Chief Scout until 2010, the Queen's representative presents individuals with the highest awards offered by the movement: The Chief Scout Award (founded by Roland Michener in 1973) and the Queen's Venturer Award.

The promise made by each member of Scouts Canada is:

> On my honour, I promise that
> I will do my best, to do my duty
> to God and the Queen
> To help other people at all times,
> and to carry out the spirit of the Scout Law.

―――――――

Crest of the Royal 22e Régiment (the Van Doos) displayed at La Citadelle. Courtesy of Christophe Finot.

RIDEAU HALL

Built in 1838, Rideau Hall one of the Queen's Canadian homes and the primary residence of the governor general. It was originally owned by Scottish stonemason Thomas MacKay. It was not until 1865 that the Ottawa residence was leased to the government as a home for Lord Monck. The property was finally purchased in 1868.

Also known as Government House, Rideau Hall has evolved in tandem with the Canadian Crown. Serving as the Sovereign's primary Canadian residence, as well as the governor general's office and residence, Rideau Hall hosts countless dignitaries, heads of state, and regular Canadians throughout the year.

———

LA CITADELLE

The largest British fortress built in North America, La Citadelle is the Queen's second Canadian home and residence of the governor general. Built between 1820 and 1850, the residence has been the home of the country's famous Francophone infantry regiment, the Royal 22e Régiment (the Van Doos), since 1920. It was Lord Dufferin who established quarters in La Citadelle in 1872, creating the tradition of governors general spending part of the year in the old capital of New France. Looking over the famous Plains of Abraham, the structure sits on the site of French fortifications that date back to the seventeenth century.

ELIZABETH THE SECOND, BY THE GRACE OF GOD OF THE UNITED KINGDOM, CANADA AND HER OTHER REALMS AND TERRITORIES QUEEN, HEAD OF THE COMMONWEALTH, DEFENDER OF THE FAITH.

TO ALL TO WHOM THESE PRESENTS SHALL COME OR WHOM THE SAME MAY IN ANYWISE CONCERN,

GREETING:

A PROCLAMATION

Deputy Attorney General

WHEREAS in and by section 4 of the National Anthem Act, being chapter 5 of the Statutes of Canada, 1980, assented to on June 27, 1980, it is provided that the said Act shall come into force on a day to be fixed by proclamation;

AND WHEREAS it is expedient that the said Act should come into force and have effect upon, from and after the first day of July, 1980.

NOW KNOW YOU that We, by and with the advice of Our Privy Council for Canada, do by this Our Proclamation declare and direct that the National Anthem Act shall come into force and have effect upon, from and after the first day of July, 1980.

OF ALL WHICH Our Loving Subjects and all others whom these Presents may concern are hereby required to take notice and to govern themselves accordingly.

IN TESTIMONY WHEREOF, We have caused these Our Letters to be made Patent and the Great Seal of Canada to be hereunto affixed.

WITNESS: Our Right Trusty and Well-beloved Edward Richard Schreyer, Chancellor and Principal Companion of Our Order of Canada, Chancellor and Commander of Our Order of Military Merit upon whom We have conferred Our Canadian Forces' Decoration, Governor General and Commander-in-Chief of Canada.

AT OTTAWA, this first day of July in the year of Our Lord one thousand nine hundred and eighty and in the twenty-ninth year of Our Reign.

By Command

Deputy Registrar General of Canada

ELISABETH DEUX, PAR LA GRÂCE DE DIEU, REINE DU ROYAUME-UNI, DU CANADA ET DE SES AUTRES ROYAUMES ET TERRITOIRES, CHEF DU COMMONWEALTH ET DÉFENSEUR DE LA FOI.

À TOUS CEUX À QUI LES PRÉSENTES PARVIENDRONT OU QU'ICELLES POURRONT DE QUELQUE MANIÈRE CONCERNER,

SALUT:

PROCLAMATION

Sous-Procureur général

ATTENDU QU' aux termes de l'article 4 de la Loi sur l'hymne national, chapitre 5 des Statuts du Canada de 1980, sanctionnée le 27 juin 1980, ladite loi entre en vigueur à la date fixée par proclamation;

ET ATTENDU QU' il est opportun que ladite loi entre en vigueur le premier juillet 1980.

SACHEZ DONC maintenant que, sur l'avis de Notre Conseil privé pour le Canada, Nous, par la présente proclamation, ordonnons que la Loi sur l'hymne national entre en vigueur le premier juillet 1980.

DE CE QUI PRÉCÈDE, Nos féaux sujets et tous ceux que les présentes peuvent concerner sont par les présentes requis de prendre connaissance et d'agir en conséquence.

EN FOI DE QUOI, Nous avons fait émettre Nos présentes lettres patentes et à icelles fait apposer le grand sceau du Canada.

TÉMOIN: Notre très fidèle et bien-aimé Edward Richard Schreyer, Chancelier et Compagnon principal de Notre Ordre du Canada, Chancelier et Commandeur de Notre Ordre du Mérite militaire à qui Nous avons décerné Notre Décoration des Forces canadiennes, Gouverneur général et Commandant en chef du Canada.

À OTTAWA, ce premier jour de juillet en l'an de grâce mil neuf cent quatre-vingt, le vingt-neuvième de Notre règne.

Par ordre

Sous-registraire général du Canada

Highlighting the relationship of authority between the Sovereign and her governor general, Governor General Edward Schreyer proclaims Canada's national anthem in the name of the Queen of Canada, 1980. Library and Archives of Canada, R1002-107-1-E.

Chapter Five

THE LIEUTENANT GOVERNORS AND THE PROVINCIAL CROWNS

As provincial representatives of the Crown, the lieutenant (pronounced *LEFT*-tenant) governors play critical roles in maintaining the balance created by Confederation. The Constitution Act, 1867, clearly lays out areas that the federal government controls (i.e., defence, money, fishing, postal service) as well as jurisdictions that the provincial governments have authority over (i.e., health, education, highways). The Queen, while being the Queen of Canada, also embodies the authority of each distinct province. This reality has led some to declare that Canada's constitutional monarchy is actually a compound monarchy of eleven Crowns (one national and ten provincial). Dr. Michael Jackson and Dr. Lynda Haverstock (former lieutenant governor of Saskatchewan) wrote in 2010:

> … the lieutenant governor is at the constitutional apex of the province, holding the royal prerogative powers in the name of the Queen. It is a crucial role. The lieutenant governor is, so to speak, the legal incarnation of provincial autonomy in Confederation.

The basis of this statement is the 1892 decision by the Judicial Committee of the British Privy Council that "… a Lieutenant Governor, when appointed, is as much the representative

The Honourable John C. Crosbie, lieutenant governor of Newfoundland and Labrador, reading the Speech from the Throne, 2010. Previous to 1779, all governors of Newfoundland were naval officers and as such resided on ships anchored in St. John's harbour during the summer months. Office of the Lieutenant Governor of Newfoundland and Labrador.

of Her Majesty for all purposes of provincial government as the Governor General himself is for all purposes of dominion government." Legally, the provincial representatives of the Crown are equivalent to the governor general, and their role in Confederation emphasizes that Canada is a partnership of equals. The Crowns of Quebec, New Brunswick, and Alberta exist to protect the autonomy of their governments. It is interesting to note that this was not the office's original purpose.

Appointed by the governor general-in-council, the office of the provincial representative of the Crown was designed by the Fathers of Confederation to be an agent of the federal government. However, over time, the status of the provinces evolved to encompass much more autonomy with respect to Ottawa. The offices of the various lieutenant governors (highlighting the flexibility of a partially unwritten constitution) developed along with the desire for increased provincial control over their own affairs. Using Quebec as an example, many people credit the provincial Crown with ensuring the survival of French culture — it

Above: The Honourable Mayann E. Francis, lieutenant governor of Nova Scotia, before entering Province House to deliver the Speech from the Throne. Her Honour is wearing the traditional civil uniform (second class) of the Queen's representative. The only other provincial representative of the Crown that still uses the civil uniform is British Columbia's lieutenant governor. Office of the Lieutenant Governor of Nova Scotia.

Left: The Honourable Steven L. Point, lieutenant governor of British Columbia. Office of the Lieutenant Governor of British Columbia.

is with the authority and protection of the Crown that such a powerful National Assembly exists in Quebec City.

Thanks to the Constitution Act, 1982, any changes to the office of the lieutenant governor (like that of the Queen and governor general) would require a resolution by the federal House of Commons, Senate, and every Legislative Assembly in the country. This ensures that the autonomy enjoyed by each province is protected by the Canadian Constitution.

————————

CONSTITUTIONAL ROLE

The lieutenant governor acts for a province as the governor general does for the country. Entrenched in the constitution, the lieutenant governor may exercise Royal prerogatives and claim the rights outlined by Walter Bagehot (the rights to be consulted, to encourage, and to warn). In fact, in looking for examples of the Royal prerogative's "reserve powers" in recent history, it is in the provinces that they have been used the most:

- Royal Assent has been withheld 112 times by the Queen's provincial representatives (assent has never been refused in the federal parliament). The last time Royal Assent was refused was by the lieutenant governor of Prince Edward Island in 1945.
- Lieutenant governors have exercised their right to reserve a bill for the governor general seventy times. The last time a provincial bill was reserved was in 1961 in Saskatchewan.
- Five premiers have been dismissed by their lieutenant governors. The last time a premier was dismissed was 1903. However, in 1991, such an action was considered by Lieutenant Governor David Lam of British Columbia.
- Lieutenant governors have refused a premier's request to dissolve a legislature three times (all in the nineteenth century).
- Lieutenant governors have several times had to exercise their judgment in the appointment of their premiers when there was no clear choice (after an

The lieutenant governor of British Columbia (The Honourable Steven Lewis Point) hosts the lieutenant governor of Alberta (The Honourable Donald Stewart Ethell) on board HMCS Calgary. The two individuals represent separate jurisdictions in their capacities as representatives of the Queen of Canada. Office of the Lieutenant Governor of British Columbia.

election, resignation, or unexpected death of their first minister). The last example of such a situation was in British Columbia with the appointment of Dan Miller as premier after the resignation of Glen Clarke in 1999.

DISTINCT CROWNS

In order to properly understand the provincial Crown, it is necessary to look at it province by province. In Saskatchewan, the Crown is a powerful symbol embraced by the government as a means of maintaining political autonomy within Confederation. However, if you look at Quebec, the Crown is not held up as a distinct provincial symbol (even though it still

The Honourable Pierre Duchesne, lieutenant governor of Quebec, takes the vice-regal salute during a 2010 Remembrance Service. Courtesy of Corporal Dom Baldwin.

has the same authority as any other provincial Crown). In Quebec, the final stage of a bill becoming law is simply called "Assent," the "Royal" having been removed decades ago.

Highlighting the role of the provincial Crown as guaranteeing the autonomy of every legislature and assembly within Confederation, each province has developed a unique relationship with its lieutenant governor.

EMBODYING THE PROVINCE IN RIGHT OF THE QUEEN

In many provinces, lieutenant governors have used their offices to highlight the richness of their provincial community. Hundreds of charitable and community organizations across Canada count the provincial representatives of the Queen as their honorary patrons, presidents, and/or members. For example, in 2010, the lieutenant governor of Prince Edward Island (Her Honour Barbara A. Hagerman) was patron of the following organizations:

- Caledonian Club of Prince Edward Island
- Canadian Cystic Fibrosis Foundation, Prince Edward Island Chapter
- Canadian Red Cross, Prince Edward Island Region
- Canadian Cancer Society, Prince Edward Island Division
- Canadian National Institute for the Blind, Prince Edward Island Division
- Canadian Parents for French (CFP), Prince Edward Island
- Federation of Canadian Music Festivals
- Fire Marshal's Office
- Girl Guides of Canada, Prince Edward Island Council
- Heart and Stroke Foundation of Prince Edward Island
- Historica Foundation of Canada
- Junior Achievement of Prince Edward Island
- Last Post Fund, Prince Edward Island Branch
- Prince Edward Island Command, Royal Canadian Legion
- Prince Edward Island Council of the Arts
- Prince Edward Island Provincial Chapter, IODE
- Prince Edward Island Rural Beautification Society
- Prince Edward Island Symphony Orchestra
- Royal Canadian Army Cadets of Prince Edward Island
- Royal Commonwealth Society of Prince Edward Island
- Seniors Active Living Centre
- Seniors College of Prince Edward Island
- The Indian River Festival

Another way in which the Crown highlights aspects of their distinct communities is through the provincial honours system discussed in Chapter Nine. However, there are also individual awards offered by the various offices — most of them unique to their home province. Some examples include:

- The Lieutenant Governor's Ontario Heritage Awards, established by the Honourable James K. Bartleman
- Lieutenant Governor's Bronze Youth Medal (Quebec)
- Lieutenant Governor's Persons with Disabilities Employer Partnership Award approved by the Honourable Mayann E. Francis (Nova Scotia)
- Lieutenant Governor's Award for Youth in Action, Youth in Motion (New Brunswick)
- Lieutenant Governor's Greenwing Conservation Award started by the Honourable John Harvard (Manitoba)
- Lieutenant Governor's Awards for Excellence in British Columbia Wines established by the Honourable Iona Campagnolo
- Lieutenant Governor's Award for Outstanding Service to Rural Saskatchewan, created by Canada Post, the Association of Rural Municipalities, and the office of Lieutenant Governor John E.N. Wiebe
- Lieutenant Governor of Alberta Arts Awards Program, founded under the patronage of the Honourable Dr. Lois E. Hole

———————

THREE-PART CROWN

In order to understand the Canadian Crown, all three of its component parts must be explored: the Queen, the governor general, and the ten lieutenant governors. There is a codependent relationship that exists between these parts: It is the Queen of Canada who gives her governors legitimacy, and it is the Queen's representatives who reinforce the Crown's local roots.

Top: The Personal Standard of the lieutenant governor of Ontario. The personal standards are flown at the various government houses and offices, and from flagpoles of buildings to indicate the presence of the lieutenant governors. Except for the standards of the lieutenant governors of Nova Scotia and Quebec, all of the provinces employ the same design shown above (except with their respective provincial shield). As the personal representative of the Sovereign, the lieutenant governor's standard takes precedence over the Canadian flag.

Middle: The Personal Standard of the lieutenant governor of Quebec

Bottom: The Personal Standard of the lieutenant governor of Nova Scotia

Chapter Six

THE CROWN IN DAY-TO-DAY LIFE

Symbols and names are an important part of a country, connecting its citizens to the roots that make their state unique in the world. Interwoven into our day-to-day lives, the symbols of the Crown of Canada provide Canadians with signposts that tell us who we are, and what makes us different as a country.

As the personification of the state, the Queen's image is reproduced on currency and stamps and is displayed across Canada in government and public institutions. Control of public lands is vested in the Queen as Crown land (89 percent of Canadian territory is owned by the federal and provincial crowns). Government copyrights are held by "The Queen in Right of Canada (or a particular province)." Public prosecutors in our legal system are called Crown attorneys (or Crown prosecutors in British Columbia, Alberta, Saskatchewan, Quebec, New Brunswick, Newfoundland and Labrador) because they represent and argue on behalf of the country (or province), which is embodied by the Queen.

The Crown is a powerful symbol of our identity and independence. Street signs, police badges, and the arms of important institutions all reflect the use of the monarchy as part of our national identity, and the Crown as the source of political authority.

There is a great depth to the Crown as a symbol of the Canadian state, highlighting a history and political structure that stretches back centuries (long before Confederation).

Dressage, *acrylic and coloured pastel on canvas, Charles Patcher, artist, 1988. When this painting was first unveiled it was controversial, but since that time has become very popular (Prince Charles requested copies to give to Princes William and Harry).* Private Collection, Toronto. ©*Charles Pachter. Reproduced by permission of the artist.*

Queen Elizabeth II Highway is one of the busiest highways in Alberta and runs from Edmonton to Calgary. Reproduced with permission by the Ministry of Transportation of Alberta.

Top Left: Royal Newfoundland Constabulary Badge. The RNC claims to have the oldest policing roots in Canada (and possibly North America) tracing its origins to a 1729 proclamation Captain Henry Osborn. The Newfoundland Constabulary was formally established in 1871, and granted permission to add the "Royal" prefix by Queen Elizabeth II in 1979. Royal Newfoundland Constabulary Headquarters.

Top Right: Lethbridge (Alberta) Regional Police badge. This badge is a rare example of one not designed by an official heraldic authority, but still being granted permission (by Queen Elizabeth II in 1966) to use the Royal Crown in its design. Lethbridge Regional Police.

Bottom: Cape Breton Regional Police Service badge. The use of the Royal Crown in this badge was the first in Atlantic Canada to receive the Sovereign's permission. Cape Breton Regional Police Service.

A great example of the Crown's use as a symbol of Canada's sovereignty can be seen along the New York State–Ontario border. The coat of arms used in New York depict the figure of Liberty (in blue) standing with a crown discarded by her left foot.

However, cross the border into Ontario and crowns are found over every highway sign in the province. In fact, the main route from Niagara Falls into Toronto is the Queen Elizabeth Way (named after the mother of Queen Elizabeth II during the 1939 Royal tour). This is a strong visual reminder of what distinguishes Canadians from Americans, in both their political structures and their separate national stories (one as a republic and the other as a constitutional monarchy).

———————

THE ROYAL PREFIX IN CANADA

Another way in which the monarchy is used to highlight the Canadian state is the use of the "Royal" prefix in the names of prominent institutions. Having "Royal" in front of an

Left: The badge of the Brandon Police Force. Brandon Police Force. Middle: The badge of the Halton Regional Police Force. The Halton Police are one of the few forces that have been presented with "Queen's Colours," representing their loyalty to the Sovereign. Halton Regional Police. *Right: The badge of the Royal Canadian Mounted Police. The use of the bison as the central image reminds Canadians that the RCMP was originally (and temporarily) established in 1873 by John A. Macdonald as the North West Mounted Police to bring order to the newly acquired western territories.* Royal Canadian Mounted Police.

© Bank of Canada / Banque du Canada

Elizabeth II's image on the twenty-dollar bill. Of all the figures depicted on Canadian currency, the Queen is the only one without an identifier.

© The Bank of Canada.

organization's name gives it a certain elevation and mystique. Such a distinction tells the public that the institution is an established part of our political and/or cultural makeup. The Royal prefix is based on specific criteria laid out by the Department of Canadian Heritage and is ultimately granted by the Sovereign. Some examples of organizations with the "Royal" prefix, with a wide range of interests and purposes, are:

- Royal Institute for the Advancement of Learning (granted in 1801 by King George III)
- Royal Canadian Academy of Arts (granted in 1880 by Queen Victoria)
- Royal Society of Canada (granted in 1882 by Queen Victoria)
- Royal Canadian Humane Association (granted in 1894 by Queen Victoria)
- Royal Astronomical Society of Canada (granted in 1903 by King Edward VII)
- Royal Canadian Mounted Police (granted in 1904 by King Edward VII)
- The Royal Architectural Institute of Canada (granted in 1908 by King Edward VII)
- Royal Naval College of Canada (granted in 1910 by King George V)
- Royal Canadian Navy (granted in 1911 by King George V, but was renamed "Maritime Command" in 1968. The original name was reinstated in 2011.)
- Royal Agricultural Winter Fair of Toronto (granted in 1920 by King George V)
- Royal Canadian Air Force (granted in 1924 by King George V, but was renamed "Air Command" in 1968. The original name was reinstated in 2011).
- Royal College of Physicians and Surgeons of Canada (granted in 1929 by King George V)
- Royal Canadian Army Cadets and Royal Canadian Sea Cadets (granted in 1942 by King George VI)
- The Royal Conservatory of Music (granted in 1947 by King George VI)

Left: The Queen Elizabeth Way, Ontario. © *Ontario Ministry of Transportation.*

Right: The King's Highway 400, Ontario. In 1930, an act was passed in Ontario changing the name of the provincial highways to "The King's Highways" (reflecting that the Sovereign at that time was King George V). This name still holds true, even though Canada has had a Queen since 1952. Since 1993, new signs have had the legend "The King's Highway" removed. © *Ontario Ministry of Transportation.*

Bottom: The coat of arms of New York State. The coat of arms of New York State depicting a discarded crown at the foot of liberty. New York State Department of State.

Above: Prince Andrew, the Duke of York, visits the Canadian Canoe Museum in Peterborough, Ontario. The Duke, patron of the museum since 2006, views the Royal Canoes (manufactured for Princess Elizabeth and Prince Philip in 1951, Prince Andrew in 1978, and Prince Charles and Lady Diana in 1981). The Duke and Duchess of Cambridge also travelled by canoe during their visit to the Northwest Territories in 2011.
Courtesy of Mollie Cartmell / The Canadian Canoe Museum.

ROYAL NOVA SCOTIA INTERNATIONAL TATTOO

Right: Logo and arms of the Royal Nova Scotia International Tattoo. The diagonal pattern in the shield reflects the intricate marching and crossovers that are done at the tattoo. The pattern is also a subtle reference to the tartans worn by tattoo participants. Royal Nova Scotia International Tattoo.

- Royal Canadian Military Institute (granted in 1948 by King George VI)
- Royal Canadian Air Cadets (granted in 1953 by Queen Elizabeth II)
- Royal Winnipeg Ballet (granted in 1953 by Queen Elizabeth II)
- Royal Canadian Geographic Society (granted in 1953 by Queen Elizabeth II)
- Royal Canadian Legion (granted in 1962 by Queen Elizabeth II)
- Royal College of Dentists of Canada (granted in 1964 by Queen Elizabeth II)
- Royal Manitoba Winter Fair (granted in 1970 by Queen Elizabeth II)
- Royal Newfoundland Constabulary (granted in 1979 by Queen Elizabeth II)
- Royal British Columbia Museum (granted in 1987 by Queen Elizabeth II)
- Royal Tyrell Museum (granted in 1990 by Queen Elizabeth II)
- Royal Saskatchewan Museum (granted in 1993 by Queen Elizabeth II)
- Royal St. John's Regatta (granted in 1993 by Queen Elizabeth II)
- Royal Heraldry Society of Canada (granted in 2002 by Queen Elizabeth II)
- Royal Alberta Museum (granted in 2005 by Queen Elizabeth II)
- Royal Nova Scotia International Tattoo (granted in 2006 by Queen Elizabeth II)
- Royal Manitoba Theatre Centre (granted in 2010 by Queen Elizabeth II)
- The Royal College of Chiropractic Sports Sciences (granted in 2010 by Queen Elizabeth II)

ROYAL PATRONS

Members of the Royal family participate directly in Canadian society by becoming active patrons (official supporters) of various organizations across the country. By giving these organizations royal patronage, the Queen and other members of the Royal family highlight their importance in Canadian society. The list of organizations is extensive; a few diverse examples are given below:

Organizations that have received patronage by the Queen:

- Canadian Cancer Society

- Canadian Medical Association
- Canadian National Exhibition Association ("The Ex")
- Canadian Naval Association
- Canadian Nurses Association
- Canadian Red Cross Society
- Save the Children Canada

Organizations that have received patronage by the Duke of Edinburgh:

- Canadian Aeronautics and Space Institute
- Dawson City Museum
- Fondation de la faune du Québec
- Naval Officers' Association of Canada
- Outward Bound Trust
- Royal Montreal Curling Club
- Royal Nova Scotia Yacht Squadron
- Royal St. Lawrence Yacht Club
- Royal Vancouver Yacht Club
- Water ski and Wakeboard Canada

Organizations which have received patronage by Prince Charles, Prince of Wales:

- Association of Canadian Underwater Councils
- Canadian Business for Social Responsibility
- Canadian Society of Landscape Architects
- Canadian Warplane Heritage Museum
- Canadian Youth Business Foundation
- Prince of Wales Northern Heritage Centre
- Regina Symphony Orchestra
- Royal Hamilton Yacht Club

Organizations that have received patronage by other members of the Royal family:

- Dundurn Castle (Duchess of Cornwall)
- Royal Alberta United Services Institute (Duke of York)
- Canadian International Air Show (Duke of York)
- Canadian Canoe Museum (Duke of York)
- The Friends of Lakefield College School (Duke of York)
- SickKids Foundation (Duke of York)
- Globe Theatre, Regina (Earl of Wessex)
- New Haven Learning Centre for Children with Autism (Countess of Wessex)
- Canadian Therapeutic Riding Association (Princess Royal)

THE DUKE OF EDINBURGH'S AWARD

The Canadian logo of the Duke of Edinburgh's Award. Duke of Edinburgh's Award Canada.

Another way in which the Canadian Crown is actively involved in the life of the country is through a variety of community awards. Perhaps the most famous of these awards is the Duke of Edinburgh's Award founded in 1956 by Prince Philip, Duke of Edinburgh (and consort to the Queen).

> … The Duke of Edinburgh's Award program propels young people on their way to overcoming challenges and achieving goals. Participants in the program have gone on to transform their own lives and those of others living at home and abroad.
>
> — Governor General Michaëlle Jean, 2010

Targeting youth, the Duke of Edinburgh's Award is a program designed to engage citizens in community service, skills, physical recreation, and adventurous journey. This award has been highly

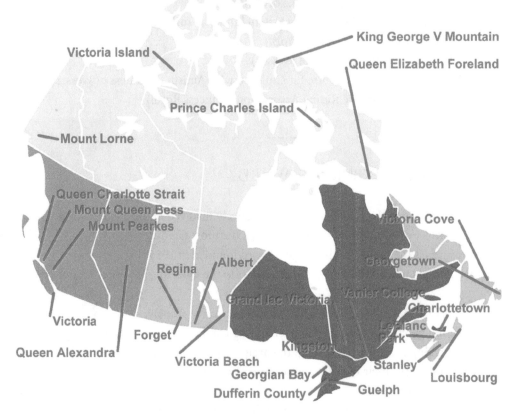

Some of the royal and vice-regal names that dot the Canadian landscape.
Image by Nathan Tidridge.

successful in partnering with schools, cadets, scouts, girl guides, colleges, and universities to reach over 37,000 young Canadians. Often Prince Philip himself or his son Prince Edward (Earl of Wessex) will distribute the program's bronze, silver, or gold badges to recipients.

NAMES

One of the main ways in which a country projects an identity is through the names given to its settlements and landmarks. Whether it is British Columbia's Mount Queen Bess (named after Queen Elizabeth I) or Ontario's Queen Elizabeth II Wildlands Provincial Park, the Crown's presence can be felt across the Canadian landscape. Not only can references to the Crown can be found in communities in every province, but they also include some the provinces themselves. Alberta is named after Princess Louise Caroline Alberta (fourth daughter of Queen Victoria and wife of Governor General the Marquess of Lorne), New Brunswick is named after the ancestral home of King George III, and Prince Edward Island is named after the fourth son of King George III (as well as the future father of Queen Victoria).

Many towns and cities carry the names of members of the Royal family, including Prince Rupert, British Columbia (nephew to King Charles I of England); Fredericton, New Brunswick (second son of King George III); Prince Albert, Saskatchewan (husband to Queen Victoria); and Arthur, Manitoba (third son of Queen Victoria).

Examples of communities named after Canadian Sovereigns and their consorts (spouses) include:

- Louisbourg, Nova Scotia (King Louis XV)
- Annapolis Royal, Nova Scotia (Queen Anne)
- Georgetown, Newfoundland (King George III)
- Kingsport, Nova Scotia (King George III)
- Kingston, Ontario (King George III)
- Georgetown, Prince Edward Island (King George III)
- Charlottetown, Prince Edward Island (Queen Charlotte)

The flag of the City of Charlottetown, Prince Edward Island. The Crown depicted on this banner of arms was the one worn by Queen Charlotte (the city's namesake), consort to King George III, at their coronation in 1761.

- Guelph, Ontario (King George IV)
- Prince William, New Brunswick (King William IV)
- Victoria, British Columbia (Queen Victoria)
- Victoria Beach, Manitoba (Queen Victoria)
- Victoriaville, Quebec (Queen Victoria)
- Regina, Saskatchewan (Queen Victoria)
- Albert, Manitoba (King Edward VII)
- Princeton, British Columbia (King Edward VII)
- Queen Alexandra, Alberta (Queen Alexandra)

As well as settlements, many of the country's natural landmarks have been named after such figures as the tragic Prince John (Mount Prince John, British Columbia), Prince Arthur (Prince Patrick Island, Northwest Territories), Princess Louise (Lake Louise, Alberta), Queen Charlotte (Queen Charlotte Strait, British Columbia) and Prince Charles (Prince Charles Island, Nunavut).

Examples of landmarks named after Canada's Sovereigns include:

- Mount Queen Bess, British Columbia (Queen Elizabeth I)
- Queen Elizabeth Foreland, Nunavut (Queen Elizabeth I)
- Lake George, New Brunswick (King George III)
- Strait of Georgia, British Columbia (King George III)
- Georgian Bay, Ontario (King George IV)
- King William Island, Nunavut (King William IV)
- Mount Victoria, Alberta (Queen Victoria)
- Grand lac Victoria, Quebec (Queen Victoria)
- Victoria Harbour, Nova Scotia (Queen Victoria)
- Victoria Cove, Newfoundland and Labrador (Queen Victoria)
- Victoria Island, Northwest Territories (Queen Victoria)
- King Edward Peak, British Columbia (King Edward VII)
- Mount Albert, Ontario (King Edward VII)
- Mount George V, British Columbia (King George V)

Château Frontenac. Governor Frontenac's coat of arms can be found throughout the hotel, including over the outside wall near the main entrance. This famous hotel was also the site of the famous Quebec Conferences of the Second World War hosted by Governor General The Earl of Athlone. Photo by Bernard Gagnon.

- King George V Mountain, Nunavut (King George V)
- Queen Elizabeth Provincial Park, Alberta (Queen Elizabeth II)
- Queen Elizabeth Islands, Northwest Territories and Nunavut (Queen Elizabeth II)

Echoes of allegiance to the Crown still exist south of the border, highlighting the fact that it was from the original thirteen states that Loyalists fled north during the American Revolutionary War. Many of the state's names reflect their origins as British colonies:

- Georgia — named after King George II
- Maryland — named after Queen Maria (consort of King Charles I)
- New York — named after the Duke of York (later King James II)

- North and South Carolina — named after King Charles I
- Virginia — named after Queen Elizabeth I (the Virgin Queen)

Emphasizing that the Canadian Crown is indeed a local institution, names used across the country also recall the representatives of the Crown. Dotted across Canadian maps are references to our governors general and lieutenant governors, including:

- Champlain Bridge, Montreal, Quebec (Samuel de Champlain)
- Champlain College, Trent University, Peterborough, Ontario (Samuel de Champlain)
- Château Frontenac, Quebec City, Quebec (Governor Louis de Buade, Comte de Frontenac)
- Amherstburg, Ontario (Governor Jeffery Amherst, first Baron of Amherst)
- Dorchester, New Brunswick (Governor General Lord Dorchester)
- Sherbrooke, Quebec (Governor General Sir John Sherbrooke)
- Parrsboro, Nova Scotia (Lieutenant Governor Colonel John Parr)
- Simcoe County, Ontario (Lieutenant Governor John Graves Simcoe)
- Dufferin County, Ontario (Governor General The Earl of Dufferin)
- Mount Lorne, Yukon (Governor General The Marquess of Lorne)
- Stanley, Nova Scotia (Governor General Lord Stanley of Preston)
- Minto City, British Columbia (Governor General The Earl of Minto)
- Grey River, Newfoundland and Labrador (Governor General The Earl Grey)
- Forget, Saskatchewan (Lieutenant Governor Amédée E. Forget)
- Willingdon, Alberta (Governor General The Viscount Willingdon of Ratton)
- Athlone, Edmonton, Alberta (Governor General The Earl of Athlone)
- Massey College, University of Toronto (Governor General Vincent Massey)
- Vanier College, Montreal (Governor General Georges Vanier)
- Grant MacEwan University, Edmonton (Lieutenant Governor Grant MacEwan)
- Mount Pearkes, British Columbia (Lieutenant Governor George Pearkes)
- Collège Jeanne-Sauvé, Winnipeg (Governor General Jeanne Sauvé)
- LeBlanc Park, Memramcook, New Brunswick (Governor General Roméo LeBlanc)

A statue of Governor General Lord Stanley is shown opening Stanley Park, Vancouver, in 1889, during the first visit by a governor general to British Columbia. Lord Stanley dedicated the park "To the use and enjoyment of people of all colours, creeds and customs for all time." The statue can be found at the main entrance to the world famous park.

The Grey Cup. This cup was originally intended to recognize the top amateur rugby football team in Canada. Canadian Football League.

- Lincoln Alexander Public School, Ontario (Lieutenant Governor Lincoln Alexander)
- Michaëlle Jean Public School, Richmond Hill (Governor General Michaëlle Jean)
- David Johnston Research and Technology Park, University of Waterloo, Ontario (Governor General David Johnston)

CULTURAL INSTITUTIONS

Some of the country's most innovative and culturally significant organizations and events were created by, or in memory of, governors general (both during and after their times in office). From the Royal Canadian Academy and the Royal Society of Canada (founded by the Marquess of Lorne in 1880 and 1882) to the Institute for Canadian Citizenship (created by Adrienne Clarkson in 2005), these institutions continue to impact Canadian society. Other important foundations and cultural events include The King's Jubilee Cancer Fund (founded by the Earl of Bessborough: this would eventually become the Canadian Cancer Society), Massey Lectures (the most important public lectures in Canada established by the CBC to honour Vincent Massey), Vanier Institute of the Family (created in 1965 by Georges Vanier), Sauvé Foundation (started by Jeanne Sauvé in 1989), Hnatyshyn Foundation (begun by Ramon Hnatyshyn), and the Michaëlle Jean Foundation (formed in 2010).

The Queen drops the puck at a Vancouver Canucks–San Jose Sharks game during her 2002 tour of Vancouver. Attending the Queen are Wayne Gretzky and Canadian Olympic hockey gold medal captains Mario Lemieux and Cassie Campbell. © Press Association.

VICE-REGAL SPORTING CUPS

As well as landmarks, perhaps the best-known connections between the vice-regal office and Canadian society are the many sporting trophies named after governors general. At the top of this list would have to be the Stanley Cup (named after Lord Stanley of Preston, who donated the cup after witnessing a hockey game in 1868), but many of Canada's top sporting awards have come to use through the representatives of the Crown:

- Minto Cup — donated by Lord Minto in 1901 and awarded to the champion junior men's lacrosse team.
- Grey Cup — donated by the Earl Grey in 1909 and awarded to the winner of the championship of the Canadian Football League.

Prince Charles and his sons, Princes William and Harry, spend time in Whistler, British Columbia, in 1998. Canada has a long history of members of the Royal family using the country as a holiday destination.
©*Press Association.*

- Devonshire Cup — donated by the Duke of Devonshire in 1918 and awarded to the champion of the Canadian Senior Golf Association.
- Lady Byng Memorial Trophy — donated by Lady Byng (wife of Governor General Lord Byng of Vimy) in 1925 and awarded by the National Hockey League to the player who exhibits the best type of sportsmanship and gentlemanly conduct combined with a high standard of playing ability of in a particular year.
- Willingdon Cup — donated by Lord Willingdon in 1927 and awarded to the winner of the Golf Canada Championship.
- Vanier Cup — donated by Georges Vanier in 1965 and awarded to the victorious team in Canadian Interuniversity Sport football.
- Jeanne Sauvé Cup — donated by Jeanne Sauvé to be presented to the champions of the National Ringette League.

Governor General Michaëlle Jean participates in an Inuit feast during a 2009 tour of Rankin Inlet, Nunavut. © Her Majesty The Queen in Right of Canada represented by the Office of the Secretary to the Governor General (2009). Sgt. Serge Gouin, Rideau Hall. Reproduced with permission of the Office of the Secretary to the Governor General.

- Ramon John Hnatyshyn Cup — donated by Ramon Hnatyshyn, this cup is presented to the winner of the Canadian International Dragon Boat Festival (founded by the Honourable David Lam, lieutenant governor of British Columbia).
- Clarkson Cup — donated by Adrienne Clarkson in 2005, the Clarkson Cup is awarded to the winner of the National Canadian Women's Hockey Championship.

PARTICIPATION IN CANADA

While this is discussed in greater detail in Chapter Eleven (Royal Tours), an important aspect of the day-to-day role of the Crown is the participation of the Queen, her family, and her representatives in Canadian activities and events. The very act of spending time in a particular place, or participating in a local, provincial, or national event involves the Crown in the life of the country.

The simple act of the Queen dropping the first puck at a Vancouver hockey game in 2002 created a thoroughly "Canadian moment" — providing a chance for Canadians to reflect on hockey as a Canadian institution. Hundreds of thousands of hockey games happen across this country, but having the Queen at one of them allowed Canadians to pause and reflect, using the spotlight that follows the Crown. Whether was Prince Charles diving into the Arctic Ocean in 1975 (emphasizing Canadian sovereignty), the Duke and Duchess of Cambridge dragon-boat racing in Prince Edward Island in 2011, or Governor General Michaëlle Jean's participation in an Inuit community feast in 2009, the mystique of the Crown provides chances to highlight and reflect on what those things mean to our country.

Chapter Seven

FIRST NATIONS AND THE CROWN

The Canadian Constitution recognizes three distinct Aboriginal groups: First Nations, Métis, and Inuit. Within these broad groups are 615 communities making up over fifty nations including:

- Tsimshian
- Nisga'a
- Anishinaabe
- Blackfoot
- Cree
- Innu
- Haudenosaunee
- Wyandot
- Mi'kmaq

It is important to recognize that each of these nations has a unique relationship with the Crown, and it has been shaped by very complicated histories stretching back centuries, some to the days of the French Crown in Canada. Samuel de Champlain was very conscious

Queen Elizabeth II talks with respected elder Sister Dorothy Moore during the 2010 tour of a Mi'kmaq cultural village marking the four hundredth anniversary of the baptism of Grand Chief Henri Membertou, the first Mi'kmaq to be baptized. Department of Canadian Heritage.

of fostering a strong bond between the French Crown and the First Nations of Canada, whom he saw as equals. Champlain referred to Aboriginal Peoples as *sauvages*, however, he meant the seventeenth-century meaning of the word which translated to "forest-dwellers."

COVENANTS

The relationships between the Crown and Canada's Aboriginal peoples are sacred and based on trust and honour. For centuries, the First Nations of Canada signed treaties with the French and British Crowns, and now with their Canadian equivalent. In total, ninety-seven treaties and final agreements have been concluded between various First Nations

Prince Charles wears a traditional Salish First Nation cedar headband and Aboriginal blanket as he receives a talking stick from The Honourable Steve Point in 2009, during a dinner hosted by the lieutenant governor at Government House in Victoria, British Columbia. Department of Canadian Heritage.

and the Crown (since 1973, and the adoption of a claims policy by the government of Canada, treaties covering nearly 40 percent of the country have been signed).

However, to refer to these agreements as merely "treaties" is to misunderstand their meaning, and many argue that they should instead be referred to as "covenants." Justice David Arnot explains that, "A covenant is ... a formal promise under oath, or an agreement that will last forever." Arnot's definition of covenant is echoed in Danny Musqua's (a Saulteaux Elder) description of Treaty No. 4 in a 1998 report, *Statement of Treaty Issues: Treaties as a Bridge to the Future*:

> We made a covenant with Her Majesty's government, and a covenant is not just a relationship between people; it's a relationship between three parties, you (the Crown) and me (First Nations) and the Creator.

The Duke and Duchess of Cambridge speak with Wendat Grand Chief Konrad Sioui as they arrive in Quebec City, July 3, 2011. The Wendat were traditional allies with the French Crown prior to the British conquest of North America in 1760.

© Press Association.

Arnot goes on to write that First Nations elders understood treaties as:

> … entering into a personal relationship — a kinship — with British subjects and most crucially, a personal relationship with the British Sovereign. The treaty was, therefore, about adoption and family within which a perpetual connection was modeled on the mutual respect and responsibilities of a family.

As the Crown evolved into a "Canadian Crown," the relationship did not change, and the treaties (i.e., covenants) have become a fundamental part of the Canadian Constitution. While presenting a tablet from the grounds of Balmoral Castle (a favourite home of Queen Victoria) to the First Nations University of Canada in 2005, Queen Elizabeth II remarked

The Queen presents a stone tablet to the First Nations University of Canada in 2005. Founded in 1976, the university has campuses in Regina, Saskatoon, and Prince Albert.

Government of Saskatchewan.

The Queen dedicates the cornerstone of the Canadian Museum for Human Rights in Winnipeg, Manitoba, during her 2010 tour of the country. Department of Canadian Heritage.

that the stone symbolized "… the foundation of the rights of First Nations peoples reflected in treaties signed with the Crown … [and] will serve as a reminder of the special relationship between the Sovereign and all First Nations people." With this message in mind, it makes sense that in 2010 the Queen dedicated the cornerstone of the Canadian Museum for Human Rights, attended by representatives of various First Nations, which contained a stone from Runnymede, England (the place where the Magna Carta was signed).

HONOUR OF THE CROWN

Treaties were entered into by Aboriginal peoples with the idea of sharing land (not surrendering it) in exchange for the protection of the Crown. These "covenants" were guaranteed by the honour of the Crown — a belief that the Crown was not an abstract idea, but a concrete person (the Queen) whose good name was reflected in the conduct of those who acted on her behalf. Surrounding the Queen were the ideals and principles of human rights that she swore to uphold as the Sovereign. Treaties remain with the Crown, emphasizing the personal relationship — or covenant — that exists between Canada's Aboriginal peoples and the Sovereign. During the 1993 talks concerning the creation of the territory of Nunavut, agreements were always made between the Inuit and "Her Majesty the Queen in Right of Canada," emphasizing the fact that this sacred relationship would still form the basis of the new territory.

The idea of the honour of the Crown was also evoked in 1990 when the Supreme Court of Canada stated that the Crown had a fiduciary (legal or ethical relationship of confidence or trust) relationship with Canada's Aboriginal peoples, placing a high burden on it (and its governments) to uphold the rights of Canada's First Nations.

QUEEN ANNE AND THE FOUR INDIAN KINGS, 1710

An example of the long relationship that the Crown has had with a particular First Nation is illustrated by a meeting between Queen Anne (reigned 1702–1714) and four First Nations chiefs in 1710. Travelling with Peter Schuyler (former mayor of Albany and a wealthy merchant), Sa Ga Yeath Qua Pieth Tow, Ho Nee Yeath Taw No Row, Tee Yee Nee Ho Ga Row (all part of the Haudenosaunee Mohawk First Nation), and Etow Oh Koam (part of the Algonquin Mohican First Nation) arrived in London, England, to petition Queen Anne for help against the French Crown. To commemorate the meeting, the Queen commissioned

Dutch artist Jan Verelst to paint each of the chiefs wearing red cloaks — gifts from Queen Anne. In addition to the cloaks, the Queen also committed to sending Anglican missionaries to the Mohawk Nation, even presenting religious instruments for use in a church built in the Mohawk Valley the following year (see section on the Chapels Royal below).

This meeting is notable for a variety of reasons. The chiefs were style as "kings" for the visit, and the Verelst paintings that were commissioned for the Queen bear the name "Four Indian Kings." This label "king" infers two things: 1. First Nations were having labels attached to them that confused their actual roles within Aboriginal societies; 2. In calling these men kings it was implied that they were equal with their European counterparts.

The historic audience between Queen Anne and the "Four Indian Kings" highlights that the relationship between First Nations and the Crown is one rooted in honour and respect that stretches back centuries. The audience is also an example of the Aboriginal peoples being accorded a status of equality by the Crown — a status that was largely ignored by succeeding governments. The American National Portrait Gallery of the Smithsonian Institute explains the portraits as "… a record of early cultural and political diplomacy between the Haudenosaunee and the British, demonstrating discourse, negotiation, and alliance."

The paintings hung at Kensington Palace (the home of Queen Anne) as part of the Royal Collection, until they were unveiled by Queen Elizabeth II at National Archives during her Silver Jubilee in 1977. To commemorate the three-hundredth anniversary of the historic audience, Queen Elizabeth II presented representatives of the Mohawk First Nation with a set of bells during her visit to St. James Cathedral in Toronto in 2010.

THE ROYAL PROCLAMATION, 1763

Issued after the conclusion of the Seven Years' War and the fall of New France, King George III's Royal Proclamation stands as the proverbial Magna Carta of Aboriginal rights in Canada:

The Royal Proclamation of 1763 was the most significant landmark in the Crown's history of treaty making with Aboriginal peoples. While not a treaty, the Proclamation did establish fundamental principles to guide the Crown in making treaties, particularly with regard to the lands of Indian nations.

The Proclamation also stands as an important recognition of the rights of Aboriginal peoples and their status as nations. It has been called the Indian Bill of Rights, and it continues to have the force of law in Canada. It is at least quasi-constitutional in nature, if not a fundamental component of the constitutional law of Canada.

(Report of the Royal Commission on Aboriginal Peoples (1996), Volume 2, Section 6.1)

The Royal Proclamation placed the Aboriginal Peoples under the direct protection of the Sovereign, ensuring that any future surrenders of land could only be made between Natives and the Crown (the Supreme Court of Canada ruled in 1997 that Aboriginal title lands could only be surrendered to the federal Crown). The Charter of the Assembly of First Nations states that the Canadian Crown is bound to honour the Royal Proclamation, affirming their right to self-government and to be members of the international community.

Originally, the Royal Proclamation only applied to the lands west of the Thirteen Colonies. Some Aboriginal peoples, like the Mi'kmaq, already had established relationships with the French Crown that were simply assumed by the new Sovereign, or had separate treaties with the British that predated the Royal Proclamation.

This portrait of King George III hangs in the Senate and was painted by Joshua Reynolds (1723–92). The Senate of Canada.

As the British colonies (and eventually Canada) expanded westward into the lands of the Hudson's Bay Company, the principles outlined in the Royal Proclamation were generally followed and resulted in a series of treaties with the Aboriginal peoples (excluding the Métis) living there.

Along the Pacific coast, many of the Aboriginal peoples had a notion of ownership or property that was similar to the Europeans and engaged in trade with them. Vancouver Island's second governor, James Douglas, began purchasing land from the First Nations for European settlement. After the election of the Vancouver Island House of Assembly in 1856, the relationships between the settlers and the First Nations rapidly deteriorated as lands were quickly seized for settlement without compensation.

In Upper Canada (modern-day Ontario), the Royal Proclamation had recognized the Great Lakes as territory of the Ojibwa, Ottawa, and Algonquin (collectively called Anishinabeg). If any future settlement was to be done in the interior of Canada, the First Nations would first have to cede their lands to the Crown.

It is important to note that the Royal Proclamation used the term "nations" when referring to some of the Aboriginal peoples, a term that disappeared in future legislation, which favoured more diminutive language such as the term "tribe."

———————

THE AMERICAN REVOLUTION

With the rebellion of the Thirteen Colonies, the various societies that made up British North America were dramatically impacted. Since all treaties and rights guaranteed to the First Nations depended on the honour of the Crown, the fact that the Americans wanted to sever their links to the Sovereign presented huge problems. Many First Nations, notably the Iroquois, fought alongside the British as allies against the American rebels (Captain Joseph Brant was commissioned as a captain in the King's Royal American Regiment). The creation of the fledgling United States of America triggered a mass migration of many First Nations who saw their future as tied to that of the Crown, heading north into lands that remained loyal to the King.

The Iroquois Confederacy was divided as half their population (approximately two thousand — the majority of whom were Mohawk, Cayuga, and Onondaga), led by Captain Joseph Brant, headed into Upper Canada and settled on land granted to them by the Crown along the Grand River. One hundred Mohawk also followed Chief John Deseronto to land granted to them on the Bay of Quinte. Knowing that the support of the Aboriginal peoples would be key in defending against any future attacks by the Americans, the Crown offered the displaced First Nations grants of land, money, and supplies.

This migration caused conflicts with the Anishinabeg (the Aboriginal peoples already living in Upper Canada) — some of whom viewed the Iroquois as their traditional enemies. Eventually the Anishinabeg (ravaged by smallpox, tuberculosis, and measles) living along the northern shoreline of Lake Ontario were persuaded to sell all the land to the Crown, which opened Upper Canada for European settlers.

Captain Joseph Brant had to travel to England to remind the British of their treaty obligations both before and after the American Revolution. The Mohawk chief was twice presented to King George III and befriended by the Prince of Wales (the future George IV).

When the War of 1812 erupted along the British North American border, the Aboriginal peoples again supported the Crown. In Upper Canada, the Shawnee Chief Tecumseh and his brother Tenskwatawa formed a powerful confederacy with the ambition of establishing an Aboriginal state in North America. With Tecumseh's death at the Battle of Moraviantown in 1813, the hopes for an independent Native country died with him. As the nineteenth century progressed, the relationship between the First Nations and the Crown deteriorated, and many of the covenants were broken.

THE INDIAN ACT, 1876

In 1876, The Indian Act was passed, authorizing the government of Canada to oversee almost every aspect of the daily lives of Aboriginal peoples. The Indian Act coincided with a tragic period of Canadian history where the official policy of the government was to assimilate its First Nations peoples. In most cases, the "covenants" established between the Crown's

Governor General Michaëlle Jean participates in the Truth and Reconciliation Commission's first national event on Indian residential schools at The Forks National Historic Site in Winnipeg, 2010. © Her Majesty The Queen in Right of Canada represented by the Office of the Secretary to the Governor General (2010). Sgt. Serge Gouin, Rideau Hall. Reproduced with permission of the Office of the Secretary to the Governor General.

ministers and Aboriginal peoples were violated by the appropriation of lands, establishment of residential schools, and untold abuses suffered by the later.

RENEWAL

Since the end of the twentieth century, the government of Canada has been trying to make amends for the behaviour of its forbearers in the hopes of restoring the honour of the Crown and renewing its covenants with the Aboriginal Peoples.

TREATY DAYS

Held throughout Canada, Treaty Days symbolically renew the covenants made between the Crown and First Nations. What a Treaty Day looks like depends on the province or territory you are in, as well as the First Nation involved. One event common to these days is the payment of a $5 annuity to every status "Indian" by the government of Canada (as promised to them by the Crown).

Many Treaty Days involve the Queen's representatives, since all treaties are between the First Nations and the Crown. Lieutenant governors of Saskatchewan have made a point of representing the Crown at most of their province's ceremonies, as do the lieutenant governors of Nova Scotia (in relation to the 1752 treaty concluded with the Mi'kmaw [Mi'kmaq] which they have attended since 1985). Speaking during the 2007 Mi'kmaw Treaty Day, the Honourable Mayann Francis emphasized the role of the modern Crown as a guarantor of a First Nation's autonomy within Canada:

> As the Queen's representative in Nova Scotia I am honoured to join with you today in celebrating the signing of the Treaty of 1752. It was a treaty of peace and friendship that ended a long war.
>
> Since it was first signed in Halifax, the treaty has come to mean much more.
>
> Today, for the Mi'kmaw people, the continuing power of this treaty — which has been affirmed by the highest court in Canada — represents the return of dignity and self-determination.
>
> The treaty that we remember today was done in the name of the Crown, King George the Second.
>
> Two hundred and fifty-five years later, I am pleased to be a link in the chain of historic continuity which has marked the relationship between the Crown and the aboriginal people of our province ... The treaty committed both sides to the rule of law ... Today, many descendants of those who signed this treaty live in communities that are experiencing a re-birth — economically, culturally and spiritually. The reaffirmation of the treaty was the catalyst for this change. It unlocked the potential of the Mi'kmaw people and set them on a new course.

―――――――――

CHAPELS ROYAL

Originally a term given to a body of priests and singers who served the spiritual needs of the Sovereign, a Chapel Royal is now an honour given to places of worship with long

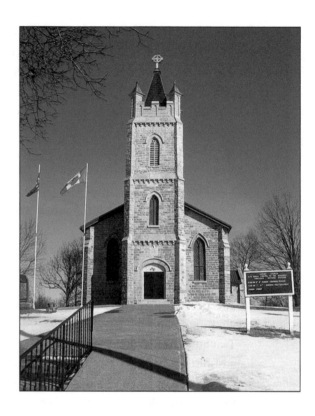

Left: Her Majesty's Royal Chapel of the Mohawk (St. Paul's) is located near Brantford, Ontario.
Photo by Norman Einstein.
Right: Her Majesty's Chapel Royal of the Mohawk (Christ Church) is near Deseronto, Ontario.
Photo by Nathan Brinklow.

and direct associations with the Crown. There are only six Chapels Royal outside of the United Kingdom and two of them are found in Canada, both of which are connected to the Mohawk First Nation.

Her Majesty's Royal Chapel of the Mohawks (St. Paul's) was built near Brantford, Ontario, by the Crown in 1785 for the Mohawk Loyalists who had fled to Upper Canada during the American Revolution. The chapel contains many artifacts from an earlier church (called the Queen Anne's Chapel) that existed in the Mohawk Valley of modern-day New York State, including a Bible and silver given to the Mohawk by Queen Anne. Given its royal designation by King Edward VII in 1904, the chapel remains one of the oldest Protestant churches in Canada.

*Governor General
Lord Tweedsmuir as
Honorary Chief Eagle
Head of the Kainai
Chieftainship. This
photograph, taken in
1937, is the work of
the legendary Canadian
photographer Yousuf
Karsh (1908–2002).
Karsh wrote of
Tweedsmuir that "He
was the most informal
of men, impatient with
the strict protocol his
position sometimes
demanded."* Yousuf Karsh,
Library and Archives of
Canada , R613-590-8-E.

Her Majesty's Chapel Royal of the Mohawk (Christ Church) was built near the Bay of Quinte in1834, replacing an older log church that had been founded by Aboriginal Loyalists. Like the chapel near Brantford, this congregation is descended from Queen Anne's Chapel of the Mohawk Valley. Queen Elizabeth II granted the chapel its royal dignity in 2004, highlighting its strong connection to the Crown. As with its Brantford counterpart, this Chapel Royal has numerous Royal artifacts highlighting its special relationship with the Crown.

Chapter Eight

THE MILITARY AND THE CROWN

It is the greatest possible privilege to wear the Canadian Navy uniform and to be made a vice-admiral. I know how busy you all are, and I cannot properly thank you enough for the service you provide. I salute you for all the work you carry out and wish you every possible success and good fortune in the future.

— Prince Charles during his visit to CFB Esquimalt Naval Base in Victoria, British Columbia.

The relationship between the Sovereign and the Canadian Forces stretches back to the very beginnings of the country. In many ways, Canada is the product of military conflicts and many of them — notably the American Revolutionary War and War of 1812 — have involved maintaining loyalty to the Crown.

———————

The badge of the Canadian Forces visually unites the former land, sea, and air forces of Canada. National Defence. Reproduced with the permission of the Minister of Public Works and Government Services, 2010.

LOYALTY

In order to enroll in the Canadian Forces, a Canadian citizen must take the following oath:

I _____ (full name), do swear (or for a solemn affirmation, "solemnly affirm") that I will be faithful and bear true allegiance to Her Majesty, Queen Elizabeth II, Queen of Canada, Her heirs and successors according to law. So help me God.

If the person enrolling is not a Canadian citizen (or British subject) a more elaborate oath is required:

I _____ (full name), do swear (or for a solemn affirmation, "solemnly affirm") that I will be faithful and bear true allegiance to Her Majesty, Queen Elizabeth II, Queen of Canada, Her heirs and successors according to law, in the Canadian Forces until lawfully released, that I will resist Her Majesty's enemies and cause Her Majesty's peace to be kept and maintained and that I will, in all matters pertaining to my service, faithfully discharge my duty. So help me God.

These are personal oaths creating a bond between the Queen and her Canadian Forces. The military is not loyal to the government of the day, but rather an individual who embodies the Canadian state. It is for these reasons that the Canadian Forces are referred to as "Her Majesty's Forces," and that a military vessel is referred to as "Her Majesty's Canadian Ship."

———

Left: A Canadian admiral's shoulder board. A shoulder board is worn on the shoulder straps of one's naval uniform and denotes rank. National Defence. Reproduced with the permission of the Minister of Public Works and Government Services, 2010.

Right: A Canadian general's epaulette has the same function as a shoulder board, but is used by the land and air forces. National Defence. Reproduced with the permission of the Minister of Public Works and Government Services, 2010.

COMMANDER-IN-CHIEF

The Queen is the commander-in-chief of the Canadian Forces, but this role is now largely exercised by the governor general (who has assumed the title "Commander-in-Chief" since 1905). Following the principles of responsible government, the commander-in-chief must follow the advice of Cabinet (Queen's Privy Council). Still, the Crown gives the role of commander-in-chief prestige, enforcing the personal connection between the Sovereign and her armed forces. By attending various military events, the Crown highlights the role that the military plays in the modern state, as well as honouring the service of its members. When King George VI and Queen Elizabeth dedicated the National War Memorial in 1939, they did so as the embodiment of the Canadian state — demonstrating both the direct relationship of the military with their King, as well as their country. Such relationships were again highlighted when Queen Elizabeth II re-dedicated the Vimy Memorial in 2007 (following in the footsteps of her uncle, King Edward VIII, who unveiled the memorial in 1936).

Left: Regiments in the Queen's realms have two flags, called colours. The junior colours represent the regiment while the senior represents the Sovereign's authority. This is the Queen's Colours of the Argyll and Sutherland Highlanders of Canada (Princess Louise's). National Defence. Reproduced with the permission of the Minister of Public Works and Government Services, 2010.

Right: Regimental Colours of the Argyll and Sutherland Highlanders of Canada (Princess Louise's). National Defence. Reproduced with the permission of the Minister of Public Works and Government Services, 2010.

COLONELS-IN-CHIEF

Adding to the personal relationship between the monarch and her armed forces, the Queen and members of her family serve as colonels-in-chief (official patrons or supporters) of a variety of military units and organizations across the country. As colonels-in-chief, the Queen and her family maintain close contacts with the members of their regiments through visits and correspondence.

The Queen is colonel-in-chief of the following units and organizations:

- 48th Highlanders of Canada (Toronto, Ontario)
- The Calgary Highlanders (Calgary, Alberta)
- The Canadian Forces School of Military Engineering

*King Edward VIII
descends from the Vimy
Ridge Memorial to greet
Canadian soldiers and
spectators in 1936.*
National Film Board of
Canada. Photothèque /
Library and Archives Canada /
PA-183542.

Queen Elizabeth II and Prince Philip, Duke of Edinburgh, walk with French Prime Minister Dominique de Villepin (left of the Queen) and Canadian Prime Minister Stephen Harper (behind the Queen) during the 2007 ceremony to mark the ninetieth anniversary of the Battle of Vimy Ridge held at the monument.
© *Press Association.*

- The Canadian Grenadier Guards (Montreal, Quebec)
- The Canadian Military Engineers Branch
- The Governor General's Foot Guards (Ottawa, Ontario)
- The Governor General's Horse Guards (Toronto, Ontario)
- The King's Own Calgary Regiment — RCAC (Calgary, Alberta)
- Le Régiment de la Chaudière (Lévis, Quebec)
- The Royal New Brunswick Regiment (Fredericton and Bathhurst, New Brunswick)
- Le Royal 22e Regiment (Quebec)

The Duke of Edinburgh is colonel-in-chief of the following units:

- The Cameron Highlanders of Ottawa (Ottawa, Ontario)
- The Queen's Own Cameron Highlanders of Canada (Winnipeg, Manitoba)
- The Royal Canadian Regiment
- The Royal Hamilton Light Infantry — Wentworth Regiment (Hamilton, Ontario)
- The Seaforth Highlanders of Canada (Vancouver, British Columbia)

The Prince of Wales is colonel-in-chief of the following units:

- Lord Strathcona's Horse — Royal Canadians (Edmonton, Alberta)
- The Air Reserve of Canada
- The Argyll and Sutherland Highlanders of Canada — Princess Louise's (Hamilton, Ontario)
- The Black Watch (Royal Highland Regiment) of Canada (Montreal, Quebec)
- The Royal Canadian Dragoons (Petawawa, Ontario)
- The Royal Regiment of Canada (Toronto, Ontario)
- The Royal Winnipeg Rifles (Winnipeg, Ontario)
- The Toronto Scottish Regiment — Queen Elizabeth The Queen Mother's Own (Toronto, Ontario)

The Princess Royal is the colonel-in-chief of the following units and organizations:

- 8th Canadian Hussars — Princess Louise's (Moncton, New Brunswick)
- Canadian Forces Communications and Electronics Branch (Kingston, Ontario)
- Canadian Forces Medical Branch

Badge of Le Regiment de la Chaudière. National Defence. Reproduced with the permission of the Minister of Public Works and Government Services, 201

Badge of the Royal Hamilton Light Infantry (Wentworth Regiment). National Defence. Reproduced with the permission of the Minister of Public Works and Government Services, 2010.

- The Grey and Simcoe Foresters (Barrie, Ontario)
- The Royal Newfoundland Regiment (St. John's and Corner Brook, Newfoundland)
- The Royal Regina Rifles (Regina, Saskatchewan)

The Duke of York is the colonel-in-chief of the following units:

- Queen's York Rangers (Toronto, Ontario)

The Earl of Wessex is the colonel-in-chief of the following units:

- Hastings and Prince Edward Regiment (Belleville, Ontario)
- Prince Edward Island Regiment (Charlottetown, Prince Edward Island)
- Saskatchewan Dragoons (Moose Jaw, Saskatchewan)

The Countess of Wessex is the colonel-in-chief of the following units:

- The Lincoln and Welland Regiment (St. Catharines, Ontario)
- The South Alberta Light Horse Regiment (Medicine Hat, Alberta)

The Duchess of Gloucester is colonel-in-chief of the following units:

- Canadian Forces Dental Services

The Duke of Kent is colonel-in-chief of the following units:

- The Lorne Scots — Peel, Dufferin, and Halton Regiment (Brampton, Ontario)

The Prince of Wales poses with the Royal Regiment of Canada at Varsity Stadium, Toronto, in 2009. The Prince had just presented new colours to the Royal Regiment of Canada and the Toronto Scottish Regiment. ©Press Association.

Top Left: Badge of Lord Strathcona's Horse — Royal Canadians. National Defence. Reproduced with the permission of the Minister of Public Works and Government Services, 2010.

Top Right: Badge of the Grey and Simcoe Foresters. National Defence. Reproduced with the permission of the Minister of Public Works and Government Services, 2010.

Bottom: Badge of the Prince Edward Island Regiment. National Defence. Reproduced with the permission of the Minister of Public Works and Government Services, 2010.

Princess Alexandra is colonel-in-chief of the following units:

- Canadian Scottish Regiment — Princess Mary's (Victoria, British Columbia)
- Queen's Own Rifles of Canada (Toronto, Ontario)

In addition to being colonels-in-chief, members of the Royal family support the military in other capacities. For example, Prince William and Prince Harry were appointed honorary Canadian Rangers in 2009, and were joined by the Duchess of Cambridge in 2011.

The Queen also holds the titles of air commodore-in-chief of the Air Reserve of Canada and captain-general of the Royal Regiment of Canadian Artillery. The Duke of Edinburgh acts as air commodore-in-chief of the Royal Canadian Air Cadets, honorary commodore of the Royal Canadian Naval Sailing Association, and admiral of the Royal Canadian Sea Cadets. On top of all of this, the Queen is patron of the Air Force Association of Canada, Royal Canadian Air Force Benevolent Fund, The Navy League of Canada, The Royal Canadian Naval Association, and The Royal Canadian Naval Benevolent Fund. Prince

King George VI and Queen Elizabeth leave after presiding over the unveiling of the National War Memorial in Ottawa in 1939. The first Royal walkabout in Commonwealth history took place on this day when the King and Queen broke with protocol and walked over to mingle with a crowd of veterans. National Film Board of Canada. Photothèque / Library and Archives Canada / C-00217.

Acting as commander-in-chief, Governor General David Johnston wears a poppy as he reviews the Prince Edward Island Regiment during a visit to Charlottetown in early November 2010. Photo by Nathan Tidridge

Charles serves as patron of the Canadian Warplane Heritage Museum, which includes one of three remaining Second World War Lancaster bombers in its vast collection.

FIRST POPPY

Inspired by John McCrae's famous poem, "In Flander's Fields," the wearing of poppies on and around Remembrance Day to remember the sacrifice of men and women in uniform is an important tradition embraced annually by Canadians since 1921 and has been adopted by member countries throughout the Commonwealth. Emphasizing the strong bond between the Crown and the Canadian Forces, each year the symbolic first national poppy is given to the governor general, while the first provincial poppies are given out to the various lieutenant governors.

Chapter Nine

THE CANADIAN HONOURS SYSTEM

Every modern country has developed ways to acknowledge the contributions of their citizens to society. The power to bestow honours is part of the Royal prerogative with the Queen as the fount (meaning spring or source) of honours for the country, meaning that it is from Her Majesty that all the honours of the Crown (both federally and provincially) flow. The concept of honour is as old as humanity itself, and the Canadian system is based on a tradition — largely British and French — that stretches back millennia.

The modern honours system can be divided into the following categories:

Orders

An Order is a society of honour that is instituted by the state. In Canada there are five national orders:

- Order of Canada (created in 1967)
- Order of Military Merit (created in 1972)
- Order of Merit of the Police Forces (created in 2000)
- Royal Victorian Order (created in 1896)

Chancellor's Chain of the Order of Canada worn by the governor general. The chain (like the other insignia of the Order of Canada) was designed by Bruce Beatty and produced by the Royal Canadian Mint. Argo Aarand enamelled the various parts of the chain using a small kiln in the basement of his home. National Defence.

- Most Venerable Order of St. John of Jerusalem (incorporated into the Canadian Honours System in 1990)

Decorations

Decorations are awarded for specific acts such as bravery, valour, gallantry, or meritorious service. Examples of Canadian decorations include the Victoria Cross, the highest decoration in the country (and whose Canadian version has yet to be awarded), and the Canadian Forces Decoration (approved by King George VI in 1950). Current members of the Royal family who hold the Canadian Forces Decoration are the Queen, the Prince of Wales, the Duke of Edinburgh, the Duke of York, the Princess Royal, the Earl of Wessex, Princess Alexandra, and the Countess Mountbatten of Burma.

Medals

Medals are awarded to commemorate service (either specific or over a long period of time), or to highlight an event of great significance to the country. The different types of medals are:

- Service medals include the Korea Voluntary Service Medal or the General Service Medal.
- Commemorative medals are struck to mark a special event (125th anniversary of Confederation), coronation, or jubilee (The Queen Elizabeth II Diamond Jubilee Medal).
- Long Service medals include the Royal Canadian Mounted Police Long Service Medal, awarded for twenty years of honourable service.
- There is a category of "other medals," which encompass such things as the Queen's Medal for Champion Shot and various provincial medals for volunteerism and citizenship.

Canadian Forces Decoration. Approved by King George VI on March 8, 1950, the decoration was unique in that it could be awarded to soldiers from all ranks. National Defence.

Top Left: Queen Elizabeth II Silver Jubilee Medal, 1977.
National Defence.

Top Right: Queen Elizabeth II Golden Jubilee Medal, 2002.
National Defence.

Bottom: Obverse and Reverse of the Queen Elizabeth II Diamond Jubilee Medal, 2012.
National Defence.

THE ORDER OF CANADA

The pre-eminent order, and foundation of the Canadian Honours System, is the Order of Canada. The idea for a uniquely Canadian national order is credited to Vincent Massey, who first introduced the idea of an Order of St. Lawrence to Governor General Lord Tweedsmuir in 1935. The idea was debated for years before it became reality — thanks partly to the famous Massey Commission and Lester Pearson, who was interested in the development of a national honour system — as the renamed Order of Canada during the 1967 Centennial celebrations. In articulating the importance of creating a national order in relation to the Canadian Crowns Father Jacques Monet explains in his introduction to *Jules Léger: A Selection of his Writings on Canada*:

> When the Rt. Hon. Roland Michener became Chancellor of the Orders of Canada and of Military Merit at the time of their institution in 1967 and 1972 respectively, the office [of governor general] acquired new responsibilities. At Rideau Hall were located the chancelleries of the two Orders and the secretariat of the Canadian system of honours ... Because of this association with Rideau Hall, and thanks to the efforts of Mr. Michener, who was in fact continuing a task first undertaken by General Vanier, the Canadian system of honours has thus remained one of the few of its kind in the world to be entirely free of partisan patronage and influence. And the Canadian Crown, as the Fount of Honour, acquired a new radiance and Canadian meaning.

The Canadian Victoria Cross was created in 1993, and has yet to be awarded. National Defence.

The Queen of Canada serves as Sovereign of the order, while the governor general is the chancellor of the order. After some initial problems, the order settled into three levels:

The Companion of the Order of Canada.
National Defence.

Companion: The highest honour that the Canadian Crown can bestow. Companions of the Order of Canada are individuals recognized for achievement and merit of the highest degree in their service to Canada or humanity at large. Since 1995, only 165 Canadians may be members of this level of the order, with a maximum of only fifteen appointed each year. Recipients are entitled to use the initials C.C. after their names.

Officer: Created in 1972, this level recognizes achievement and merit made by an individual to a high degree of service to Canada or humanity at large. Membership to this level is not capped, but a maximum of seventy-five appointments can be made each year. Recipients are entitled to use the initials O.C. after their names.

Member: Added in 1972, 136 people can be appointed to this level of the Order of Canada each year. Recognizing distinguished service in a particular locality, group, or field of activity, there is no limit to the amount of members this level can have. Recipients are entitled to use the initials C.M. after their names.

THE ORDER OF MILITARY MERIT

Like the Order of Canada, the Order of Military Merit has the Queen of Canada as its Sovereign. Rather than chancellor, the governor general is styled as the principal commander. The three levels of the order include:

Commander: Awarded to individuals holding the rank of brigadier general/commodore or higher, this level recognizes outstanding meritorious service in duties of great responsibility. Recipients are entitled to use the initials C.C.M. after their names.

Officer: Primarily awarded to officers between the ranks of major and colonel, this level also recognizes outstanding meritorious service in duties of great responsibility. Recipients are entitled to use the initials O.M.M. after their names.

Member: Recognizing exceptional service and performance of duty, this level is awarded to individuals from non-commissioned ranks and junior officers below the rank of major/lieutenant commander. Recipients are entitled to use the initials M.M.M. after their names.

ORDER OF MERIT OF THE POLICE FORCES

Canada is one of the few countries with a separate order to recognize the achievements of its police forces. Established by the Queen in 2000, the order also includes the standard three levels:

Commander: Recognizing outstanding meritorious service and leadership in duties of great responsibility over an extended period of time, recipients are entitled to use the initials C.O.M. after their names.

Officer: An Officer has demonstrated meritorious service over an extended period of time, and is entitled to use the initials O.O.M. after their name.

Member: Appointed for exceptional service, or performance of duty over an extended period of time, members are entitled to use the initials M.O.M. after their names.

THE QUEEN'S PERSONAL HONOURS

These honours are given to Canadians at the personal direction of the Sovereign (without government influence or interference). The Queen's personal honours allow the monarch to recognize individuals who have served the Crown directly, and typically these names are submitted to her by the Queen's Canadian Secretary. In her ability to personally honour Canadians, the Queen has four separate honours at her disposal:

Member of the Order of Military Merit. National Defence.

Former prime minister Jean Chrétien after being presented with the Order of Merit by the Queen on July 13, 2009. His wife Aline Chrétien stands with him. © Press Association.

The Order of Merit

Founded by King Edward VII in 1902, this is the most exclusive non-titular honour (meaning it does not come with a title) in the Commonwealth. Limited to twenty-four living members, the Order of Merit is for individuals who have given exceptional meritorious service of international magnitude. Only four Canadians have been appointed to this prestigious Order: The Right Honourable William Lyon Mackenzie King (1947), Colonel Dr. Wilder Penfield (1953), The Right Honourable Lester B. Pearson (1971), and The Right Honourable Jean Chrétien (2009).

The Royal Victorian Chain

Also established by King Edward VII in 1902, the Royal Victorian Chain is presented to individuals whom the Sovereign holds in great esteem and affection. Two Canadians have been honoured this way: The Right Honourable Vincent Massey (1960) and The Right Honourable Roland Michener (1974).

The Royal Victorian Order

Founded by Queen Victoria in 1896, the Royal Victorian Order is given to individuals who have done extraordinary and/or personal service to the Sovereign or members of the Royal family. While there are five levels to this order, Canadians are not eligible for the top two because they carry titles with them (Canadians have traditionally not been allowed to accepted "titled" honours since 1935). The levels available to Canadians are Commander, Lieutenant, and Member.

The Royal Victorian Medal

Also created by Queen Victoria in 1896, the medal is used to honour members of the Royal Households and Government Houses, as well as junior civil servants and non-commissioned members of the Canadian Forces.

Member of the Royal Victorian Order. There is no set criteria for this order and it is awarded entirely at the discretion of the Sovereign. National Defence.

THE MOST VENERABLE ORDER OF THE HOSPITAL OF ST. JOHN OF JERUSALEM

Associated with North America since the early days of New France and Acadia, the Most Venerable Order of the Hospital of St. John of Jerusalem has a rich history in this country. Abandoned after the fall of New France, the order returned to Canada informally in 1883 when it administered a first-aid course in Quebec City. Canadians have been appointed to the Order of St. John since 1883 when it became a recognized order of chivalry by Queen Victoria. As with the other national honours, the Queen is Sovereign of the order and, since 1946, the governor general has served as prior. All levels of the order are awarded to Canadians who have performed good service for the order while following its established rules. Typically, recipients are expected to move up through the ranks, although there are no set criteria for each level.

Levels of the Most Venerable Order of the Hospital of St. John of Jerusalem:

- Bailiff or Dame Grand Cross
- Knight or Dame of Grace or Justice
- Commander
- Officer
- Member

PROVINCIAL HONOURS

Since they are Sovereign entities within the jurisdictions laid out by the Constitution Act 1867, Canadian provinces have developed their own honours that are largely recognized by the federal government. Quebec is credited with developing the first provincial honour in 1889 with the founding of the Agricultural Merit Awards (this was later developed into the Order of Agricultural Merit in 1925).

PROVINCIAL ORDERS

For a long time, lieutenant governors lobbied to be made ex-officio (a member of a body who is part of it because they hold a high office) members of the Order of Canada. Their requests denied, the door was opened for the creation of a series of independent provincial honours. Alberta became the first to create a provincial order with the founding of the Alberta Order of Excellence in 1979. Quebec, Saskatchewan, Ontario, and British Columbia soon followed. By 1991, the provincial orders were recognized by the federal government and added to the Canadian order of precedence (a symbolic hierarchy of positions highlighting the importance of various Canadian honours), leading to the creation of orders by all the remaining members of Confederation.

Provincial Orders:

The Alberta Order of Excellence (1979). National Defence.

L'Ordre national du Québec — officer (1984). National Defence.

The Saskatchewan Order of Merit (1985). National Defence.

Order of Ontario (1986). National Defence.

Order of British Columbia (1989). National Defence.

The Order of Prince Edward Island (1997). National Defence.

The Order of Manitoba (1999). National Defence.

The Order of New Brunswick (2000). National Defence.

The Order of Nova Scotia (2001). National Defence.

The Order of Newfoundland and Labrador (2001). This order is the only Canadian honour that uses stone in its insignia's design. National Defence.

Each order has specific criteria, but in general they recognize the highest service to their home province. With the exception of Quebec, every lieutenant governor serves as chancellor of their provincial order, and appointments are made by the lieutenant governor-in-council. Unlike the Order of Canada, the Queen does not serve as Sovereign of any provincial honour although all (excepting Quebec, Alberta, and Prince Edward Island) have permission to use the Royal Crown on their insignia.

Chapter Ten

THE CANADIAN HERALDIC AUTHORITY

Throughout this book are examples of the ancient art of Canadian heraldry. One of the royal prerogatives of the Crown is the ability to grant such arms to institutions and individuals across the country. The granting of arms is an ancient tradition that grew out of medieval Europe and the need to distinguish competing knights at various tournaments. Since knights were completely covered in armour, the practice developed of painting specific symbols on their shields in order to identify them to the onlookers. Eventually, certain symbols became associated with certain individuals and a way to avoid identical devices being used by two different people was needed. The subject popularly called heraldry (but properly, armory) was born.

———

HERALDS

Medieval tournaments were sponsored by kings, queens, and other important nobles who would turn the actual task of organizing the events over to a herald. As the official announcer of a particular tournament, the heralds had to familiarize themselves with the

Her Majesty Queen Elizabeth II witnessing the unveiling of the new arms and badge of the Canadian Border Services Agency. With the Queen (and wearing her chain of office) is Claire Boudreau, chief herald of Canada. ©*Her Majesty in Right of Canada as administered by the Canadian Heraldic Authority 2010*

various devices used by knights. Over time, the heralds became experts in identifying who was who, and as more and more knights began to use symbols, they went to their local heralds for advice. Eventually, in an effort to regulate the creation of new symbols, or arms, the power to grant them was assumed by Europe's monarchs, and managed by the heralds.

In Canada, any person can be honoured by the Crown by being granted a coat of arms.

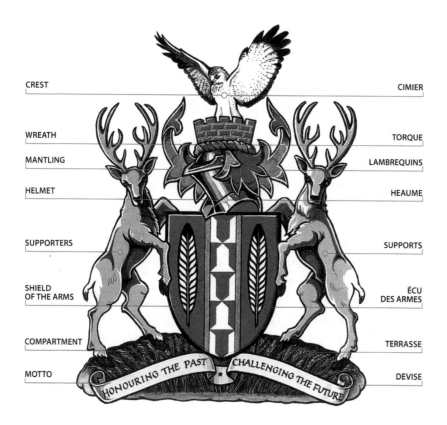

CREST — CIMIER

WREATH — TORQUE

MANTLING — LAMBREQUINS

HELMET — HEAUME

SUPPORTERS — SUPPORTS

SHIELD OF THE ARMS — ÉCU DES ARMES

COMPARTMENT — TERRASSE

MOTTO — DEVISE

HONOURING THE PAST CHALLENGING THE FUTURE

THE COAT OF ARMS OF THE | LES ARMOIRIES DU

Town of Penhold, Alberta

The arms of the Town of Penhold, Alberta. ©*Her Majesty in Right of Canada as administered by the Canadian Heraldic Authority 2010.*

COMPONENTS OF A GRANT OF ARMORIAL BEARINGS (A.K.A. COAT OF ARMS)

Crest: The crest developed from a fan-shaped metal plate that appeared on knights' helmets as a way to deflect a blow to the head.

Wreath: A twisted silk cloth that originally hid the gap between the helmet and the crest. In heraldry, the wreath is typically in the two main colours of the arms.

Mantling: Originally a cloth that hung over the shoulders to deflect the sun, mantling is a flourish used to highlight the principle colours of the arms.

Helmet: Originally, the heralds only recorded the shields, but as heraldry evolved, different helmets were added. Different helmets denoted rank and class, but in Canada the only special helmet is for the Sovereign. It is a gold front-facing and barred helmet.

Supporters: Emerging during the fifteenth century, various supporters (animals and/or people) were added to grants of arms. Denoting rank, supporters are restricted in Canada to be used by corporate bodies, governors general, lieutenant governors, privy councillors, and other eminent Canadians.

Shield of the Arms: The most important part of a grant, the arms are simple and easily identifiable from a distance. The shape of the actual shield is left to the artist who also makes use of a variety of images and colours to create the image, but must adhere to the rules of heraldry that have developed over the centuries. One of these rules limits the herald to using five base "colours" and two "metals," collectively called "tinctures," in their designs:

Colours:
Red — Gules
Blue — Azure
Green — Vert
Black — Sable
Purple — Purpure

Painting to accompany
Letters Patent granting
Armorial Bearings to

Dessin annexé aux
lettres patentes de concession
d'emblèmes héraldiques à

THE WATERDOWN - EAST FLAMBOROUGH
HERITAGE SOCIETY
WATERDOWN, ONTARIO

As entered in
Volume VI, page 43 of the
Public Register of Arms, Flags
and Badges of Canada,
this 15th day of April 2011.

Tel que consigné dans
le volume VI, page 43 du
Registre public des armoiries,
drapeaux et insignes du Canada,
ce 15ᵉ jour d'avril 2011.

Herald Chancellor

Chancelier d'armes

Chief Herald of Canada

Canada

Héraut d'armes du Canada

Deputy Herald Chancellor

Vice-chancelier d'armes

The artwork from the patent of arms of The Waterdown—East Flamborough Heritage Society (Ontario) granted in April 15, 2011. In an effort to preserve their local heritage for future generations, a committee was struck to work with the Saguenay Herald to create a grant of arms and a flag that reflected the historic Town of Flamborough, which was dissolved in 2001. Pictured are the arms, flag, and badge granted to the society.
Courtesy of the Waterdown-East Flamborough Heritage Society.

Metals:

Silver — Argent (generally represented as white)

Gold — Or

In order to meet the demands of more and more petitions for arms, heralds developed a wide variety of artistic patterns, partitions, and furs to use in their designs. Also, a wide variety of images (called "devices") have evolved, including the use of animals, heraldic beasts, flowers, trees, weapons, and various body parts. As the art of heraldry evolves in this country, many more devices are being used, including those unique to Canada such as bison, huskies, narwhals, and polar bears.

Compartment: The area in which the supporters stand has been used to highlight symbols — typically found in the natural environment — that cannot be used in the shield of arms.

Motto: A phrase or saying associated with the individual or body being granted the arms. Often written in Latin, Canadian mottos have also been depicted in English, French, and even Inuktitut (The Arms of Nunavut).

BACKGROUND ON THE CANADIAN HERALDIC AUTHORITY

The art of heraldry was brought to Canada with the European explorers and settlers during the fifteenth and sixteenth centuries. Canadians had to petition the College of Arms in England or the Court of Lord Lyon in Scotland if they wanted their own distinct grants of arms. This process changed on June 4, 1988, when Queen Elizabeth II authorized the governor general to exercise her royal prerogative of granting arms. Since then, the Canadian Heraldic Authority has granted arms to Canadians in the name of the Queen of Canada, as represented by the governor general.

Canadians now petition the Chief Herald of Canada, who is part of Rideau Hall's (Government House) Chancellery of Honours, for a grant of arms. If accepted, the chief herald will ask the deputy herald chancellor (the deputy secretary to the governor general) for an official warrant. When the warrant is approved, the file is sent to one of the heralds who work in the office to develop the actual coat of arms. Different for every applicant, the process of being granted a coat of arms typically takes a year from start to finish.

ARMS OF THE CANADIAN HERALDIC AUTHORITY

Granted in 1993, the armorial bearings of the Canadian Heraldic Authority, in true fashion, provide a visual explanation of the institution's role in our society. The description given by the Authority explains:

> The shield features the maple leaf of Canada charged with a smaller shield, which indicates the heraldic responsibilities of the Authority.
>
> The crest consists of the crowned lion resting its paw on a shield, symbolizing the fact that the Governor General is the head of the Authority and that heraldic emblems are honours flowing from the Canadian Crown.
>
> The supporters are special heraldic beasts, half raven and half polar bear. Many First nations in Canada regard the raven as a creator or transformer, while the polar bear is known for its strength and endurance. These supporters represent the responsibility of Canada's heralds to create symbols for a wide range of Canadian institutions and individuals. The supporters rest on an outcrop of the Canadian Shield, representing the solid foundations on which the Authority has been established.
>
> The Latin motto can be translated as: Let those who honour their country be honoured.

Arms of the Canadian Heraldic Authority.
©Her Majesty in Right of Canada as administered by the Canadian Heraldic Authority 2010.

The Baton of the Chief Herald of Canada. ©Her Majesty in Right of Canada as administered by the Canadian Heraldic Authority 2010.

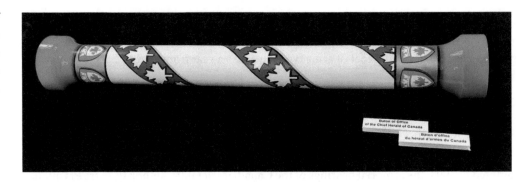

BADGES OF OFFICE

Left: Herald Chancellors: Léopold Amyot (1988–90), Judith Ann Larocque (1990–2000), Barbara Uteck (2000–06), Sheila-Marie Cook (2006–11), and Stephen Wallace (2011–present). ©Her Majesty in Right of Canada as administered by the Canadian Heraldic Authority 2010.

Canada's heralds and officers within the Authority have their own distinct badges to represent them.

Right: Chief Herald of Canada, Robert D. Watt (1988–2007), Claire Boudreau (2007–present). ©Her Majesty in Right of Canada as administered by the Canadian Heraldic Authority 2010.

Following the tradition of heraldry, Canadian heralds take their names from rivers within the country, although their service is not limited to a particular area.

Top Left: Saint-Laurent Herald Auguste Vochon (1988–2000), Claire Boudreau (2000–07), and Bruce Patterson (2008–present). ©Her Majesty in Right of Canada as administered by the Canadian Heraldic Authority 2010.

Top Right: Athabaska Herald Charles Maier (1988–2001). ©Her Majesty in Right of Canada as administered by the Canadian Heraldic Authority 2010.

Bottom Left: Fraser Herald Cathy Bursey-Sabourin (1989–present). ©Her Majesty in Right of Canada as administered by the Canadian Heraldic Authority 2010.

Bottom Right: Saguenay Heralds: Claire Boudreau (1997–2000), Bruce Patterson (2000–08), Karine Constantineau (2008–09), and Forrest Pass (2009–present). © Her Majesty in Right of Canada as administered by the Canadian Heraldic Authority 2010

Top Left: Assiniboine Herald Darrel Kennedy (2000–01, 2002– present) ©Her Majesty in Right of Canada as administered by the Canadian Heraldic Authority 2010.

Top Right: Miramichi Heralds: Karine Constantineau (2003– 08) and Monan Labelle (2009–present). ©Her Majesty in Right of Canada as administered by the Canadian Heraldic Authority 2010.

Bottom: Coppermine Herald Catherine Fitzpatrick (2003– present). ©Her Majesty in Right of Canada as administered by the Canadian Heraldic Authority 2010.

Chapter Eleven

ROYAL AND VICE-REGAL TOURS

… an enormous amount of effort has always gone in to the tours and events the Queen or the governor general [or lieutenant governor] attends. Their presence is often the glorious culmination of years of fund-raising, community organization, and major service commitment. The visit brings honour and dignity to quiet but substantial achievement and volunteer efforts. The pride of accomplishment the local community takes in a royal or vice-regal visit is hard to quantify or otherwise describe in a news story, which is why you seldom read about them, but it is real nevertheless.

— John Fraser, *Eminent Canadians*

A Royal tour has the effect of placing a magnifying glass on Canadian society (whether it is national, provincial, or local). Tours are used by governments to highlight significant milestones and/or achievements in the life of the country. By having the Queen (or a member of her family) at a particular event, a high level of media coverage and public interest are assured. Usually planned by the Canadian Secretary to the Queen, Royal

The official badge of the 2010 Royal tour of Queen Elizabeth II and the Duke of Edinburgh. © Her Majesty in Right of Canada as administered by the Canadian Heraldic Authority 2010.

Edward, Prince of Wales, and future King Edward VIII, canoes on the Nipigon River in northwestern Ontario in 1919. The Prince spent three days (September 5–8) out in the wilderness, canoeing, fishing, and hiking. On September 7, the Prince was nearly crushed by a tree blown over during a fierce thunderstorm.
Library and Archives of Canada, PA-022366.

tours can take months (and sometimes years) to put together, usually encompassing a larger theme agreed upon by the Queen or other member of the Royal family (the theme of the 2010 Royal tour was "The Canadian Record of Service" while the Duke and Duchess's 2011 Royal tour was "Moving Forward Together").

Royal Tours by the Queen and Prince Philip:

- 1957: October 12–14. To open the first session of the twenty-third Parliament in Ottawa (also visited Hull).
- 1959: June 18–August 1. Toured every province and territory of Canada, as well as opened the St. Lawrence Seaway.
- 1964: Oct. 5–13. Commemorated Charlottetown and Quebec conferences by visiting Charlottetown, Quebec City, and Ottawa.
- 1967: June 29–July 5. To commemorate the centennial of Confederation, as well as visit Expo '67 in Montreal.

- 1970: July 5–15. Accompanied by Prince Charles and Princess Anne, the Queen and Prince Philip toured the Manitoban communities of Churchill, Thompson, Gillan, Flin Flon, Norway House, Swan River, The Pas, Dauphin, Clear Lake, Brandon, Baily Farm, Portage la Prairie, Oakville, Winnipeg, Carman, Beausejour, Lower Fort Garry to mark the one hundredth anniversary of Manitoba's entry into Confederation. The Royal family also visited the Northwest Territories to participate in their centennial celebrations.
- 1971: May 3–12. Accompanied by Princess Anne, the Queen and Prince Philip toured the British Columbia communities of Victoria, Vancouver, Tofino, Kelowna, Vernon, Penticton, Williams Lake, and Comox to mark the centenary of British Columbia's entry into Confederation.
- 1973: June 25–July 5. Toured the Ontario communities of Toronto, Cobourg, Kingston (celebrating their three hundredth anniversary), Cambridge, Kitchener, Waterloo, London, St. Catharines, Niagara-on-the-Lake, Scarborough, Brampton, and Milton. Celebrated the centennial of Prince Edward Island's entry into Confederation by touring Charlottetown, Summerside, and Mount Carmel. Toured Regina, Saskatchewan, and Calgary, Alberta, to participate in events marking the centenary of the Royal Canadian Mounted Police.
- 1973: July 31–August 4. Opened the Commonwealth Heads of Government meeting in Ottawa, Ontario.
- 1976: July 13–25. Joined by Prince Charles, Prince Andrew and Prince Edward attended the XXI Olympic Games in Montreal (which the Queen opened).
- 1977: Oct. 14–19. Time spent in Ottawa to mark the Queen's Silver Jubilee Year.
- 1978: July 26–August 6. Joined by Prince Andrew and Prince Edward, the Queen and Prince Philip toured the Newfoundland and Labrador communities of St. John's, Deer Lake, Strawberry Hill, Corner Brook, and Stephenville Airport. They also visited the Saskatchewan communities of Regina, Yorkton, Fort Qu'Appelle, Balcarres, Melville, Moose Jaw, Saskatoon, Lloydminster, and the Albertan communities of Edmonton (where the Queen opened the XI Commonwealth Games), Grande Prairie, Peace River, St. Paul, Vegreville, Fort Saskatchewan, Mundare, Chipman, Lamont, Bruderheim, and Fort Edmonton.

- 1982: April 15–19. Proclaimed the Constitution Act, 1982, in Ottawa.
- 1983: March 8–11. Toured British Columbia communities of Victoria, Vancouver, Nanaimo, Vernon, Kamloops, and New Westminster.
- 1984: Sept. 24–October 7. Marked the bicentennial of New Brunswick by touring Dieppe, Shediac, Moncton, Fredericton, Sackville, and Riverview. The Royal couple also celebrated the bicentennial of Ontario by touring Ottawa, Morrisburg, Cornwall, Prescott, Kingston, Amherstview, Windsor, Brantford, and Sudbury. After Sudbury, the Queen alone continued into Manitoba to tour through Winnipeg, Dauphin, Brandon, and Dugald.
- 1987: October 9–24. Opened the Commonwealth Heads of Government meeting in Victoria and Vancouver, British Columbia. Toured Regina, Fort Qu'Appelle, Saskatoon, Yorkton, Canora, Veregin, Kamsack, Kindersley, in Saskatchewan, before moving on to Quebec City, Sillery, Cap Tourmente, Rivière-du-Loup, La Pocatière in Quebec.
- 1990: June 27–July 1. Toured solo through Calgary and Red Deer, Alberta, as well as Ottawa.
- 1992: June 30– July 2. Marked the 125th anniversary of Confederation and the fortieth anniversary of her accession in Ottawa and Hull.
- 1994: August 13–22.Toured the Nova Scotia communities of Halifax, Sydney, Fortress of Louisbourg, and Dartmouth before heading to Victoria, British Columbia, to open the Commonwealth Games. Also visited Yellowknife, Rankin Inlet, and Iqaluit.
- 1997: June 23–July 2. Also toured the Newfoundland and Labrador communities of St. John's, Gander, Bonavista (to mark the four hundredth anniversary of the arrival of John Cabot's vessel, *The Matthew*), North West River, Sheshatshiu, and Happy Valley-Goose Bay. They also toured the Ontario communities of London, Stratford, Brantford, Toronto, North Bay, Petawawa, and Ottawa. Prince Philip flew to Manitoba to view the damage caused by the flooding in the Red River Valley.
- 2002: October 4–15. Marked the Queen's Golden Jubilee by touring Iqaluit (Nunavut), Victoria and Vancouver (British Columbia), Winnipeg (Manitoba),

The Duke and Duchess of Cambridge tour the devastated Albertan community of Slave Lake in 2011. By visiting the region, the Duke and Duchess brought with them nearly 1,500 members of the media that highlighted the damage caused by forest fires to this remote town. The tour also boosted the morale of the residents, re-emphasizing that they were in the minds of all Canadians. Department of Canadian Heritage.

Toronto, Oakville, and Hamilton (Ontario), Fredericton, Sussex, and Moncton (New Brunswick), as well as Ottawa.

- 2005: May 17–25. Marked the centennials of Saskatchewan and Alberta by touring Regina and Saskatoon (Saskatchewan), and Jasper, Edmonton, Fort McMurray, and Calgary (Alberta).

- 2010: June 28– July 6. Toured Halifax, Nova Scotia, where the Queen participated in an International Fleet Review to mark the one hundredth anniversary of the Royal Canadian Navy. The Queen and Prince Philip also visited Ottawa before moving on to Manitoba to lay the keystone for the Canadian Museum for Human Rights in Winnipeg. Afterwards, the Queen toured through Ontario communities of Toronto and Waterloo.

Tours and visits by other members of the Royal family:

- Prince Philip (without the Queen): 1959, 1960, 1962, 1966, 1967 (multiple), 1969, 1974, 1975, 1977, 1978 (multiple), 1979, 1980 (multiple), 1983 (multiple), 1984, 1985 (multiple), 1987, 1989 (multiple), 1990, 1992 (multiple), 1993, 1996, 1997, 1998, 2001, and 2004.
- Prince Charles: 1970, 1975 (multiple), 1976, 1977, 1979, 1980, 1982, 1983, 1986, 1991, 1996, 1998, 2001, and 2009.
- Princess Anne: 1970, 1971, 1974, 1979, 1982, 1986, 1988, 1991, 1998, 1999, 2003, 2004, 2007, and 2010 (multiple).
- Prince Andrew: 1976, 1977, 1978, 1983, 1985, 1987 (multiple), 1991, 1992, 1993, 1995, 1997, 1999, 2000, 2001, 2003 (multiple), 2007 (multiple), 2008 (multiple), and 2009 (multiple).
- Prince Edward: 1976, 1978, 1987, 1988, 1989, 1990, 1991, 1992, 1993 (multiple), 1994, 1996, 1999, 2000 (multiple), 2001, 2002 (multiple), 2003, 2005, 2006, 2007, 2008, 2009, and 2010.
- Prince William: 1991, 1998, and 2011 (with the Duchess of Cambridge).

VICE-REGAL TOURS OF CANADA

The governor general spends a lot of their mandate visiting as much of the country as possible, as the representative of the Queen. Vice-regal tours (like Royal tours) highlight the various communities, events, histories, and individuals that make up Canadian federation.

For example, here is the itinerary of Governor General David Johnston's first official visit to Ontario:

Thursday, December 2
Toronto, Ontario
12:00 p.m.
16th Annual Association of Fundraising Professionals Greater Toronto
Chapter's Philanthropy Awards Luncheon
His Excellency will address award recipients and guests at the 16th Annual
Association of Fundraising Professionals (AFP) Greater Toronto Chapter's
Philanthropy Awards ceremony.

3:00 p.m.
Official Welcoming Ceremony at the Legislative Assembly of Ontario
Upon their arrival at the Legislative Building at Queen's Park, Their
Excellencies will be greeted by the Honourable Dalton McGuinty, Premier
of Ontario; the Honourable Steve Peters, Speaker of the Legislative
Assembly of Ontario; and His Honour David C. Onley, Lieutenant
Governor of Ontario. The Governor General will receive full military
honours, which will include a 21-gun salute, the "Viceregal Salute" and
the inspection of the guard of honour, composed of soldiers from the 32
Canadian Brigade Group and the Governor General's Horse Guards.

3:30 p.m.
Meeting with the Honourable Dalton McGuinty, Premier of Ontario
Premier's Office, Queen's Park, Toronto

4:00 p.m.
Governor General to Address Members of the Legislative Assembly of
Ontario

6:30 p.m.
Reception Hosted by the Premier of Ontario
In honour of Their Excellencies' official visit to Ontario, the Premier will

host a reception during which they will have the opportunity to meet and speak with Ontarians who have contributed to their communities. The Governor General will deliver a speech on this occasion.

Friday, December 3
Toronto, Ontario
8:30 a.m.
Visit to the Holland Bloorview Kids Rehabilitation Hospital
On the occasion of the International Day of Persons with Disabilities, Their Excellencies, along with Their Honours the Honourable David C. Onley, Lieutenant Governor of Ontario, and Mrs. Ruth Ann Onley, will visit Holland Bloorview Kids Rehabilitation Hospital, Canada's largest children's rehabilitation teaching hospital, fully affiliated with the University of Toronto.

10:15 a.m.
Visit to Dewson Street Junior Public School
Their Excellencies will visit this successful downtown school. They will read books to the children and participate in a question period with students.

11:30 a.m.
Meeting with His Worship Rob Ford, Mayor of Toronto
Their Excellencies will be greeted by Mayor Rob Ford at the main doors of the City Hall where they will walk past a guard of honour of members of Toronto EMS, Toronto Fire Service, the Toronto Police Service, the Toronto Transit Commission and City staff. Their Excellencies will also sign the official guest book.

VICE-REGAL VISITS TO FOREIGN COUNTRIES

Beginning with the visit by Governor General Lord Willingdon to the United States in 1927, there has been a long tradition of vice-regal visits to foreign countries. Since they represent the Queen, governors general are accorded the same protocol as a head of state when they are abroad. The first full Canadian State Visit (a visit that is accorded the pomp and ceremony required to represent the dignity and respect due to a visiting state) took place in 1937, when Governor General Lord Tweedsmuir travelled to the United States to address their Senate.

Official overseas visits are always at the request of the Canadian government or the invitation of a host government or organization. These visits are very important in developing Canada's relationships with foreign governments and organizations and have become an important role of the Queen's representative.

Between 2009 and 2010, Governor General Michaëlle Jean visited twelve countries. The *Annual Report of the Office of the Secretary to the Governor General* highlights the importance of these overseas visits as it outlines the State visits to the Ukraine and the Kingdom of Norway:

> The State visit to Ukraine highlighted Canada's ongoing support for the country's democratic transformation and economic reforms, as well as the strength of our historic ties and partnerships that connect Canada and Ukraine. In Norway, the visit helped to further develop bilateral relations between the two countries. The visit also underscored our shared values, including the importance we place on finding a fair balance between economic development and environmental protection, and the priority we give to education and youth engagement. This State visit also provided an opportunity for Canada and Norway to pool their expertise on Arctic development and northern populations. During these visits, the Governor General took part in various ways by:
>
> • holding talks with the heads of State, as well as with the heads of government and other legislators, during private meetings, State dinners and courtesy calls in each of the two countries;

- participating in forums and panel discussions with youth groups, academics, community leaders and local non-governmental organizations on subjects such as governance and the role of civil society, civic engagement, inclusive education, diversity, and achievements in the cultural sector;
- participating in a discussion with Ukrainian women on the challenges and opportunities they face in the political, economic and health spheres;
- promoting the benefits of economic collaboration during a luncheon attended by the Canadian Ukrainian community and the Canadian Business Club in Ukraine and during a meeting with Canadian and Norwegian business people to discuss what businesses can do to mitigate the negative effects of climate change;
- attending a reception with members of the Canadian and Norwegian community featuring acclaimed Canadian soprano singer Measha Brueggergosman and highlighting the 2010 Winter Olympic Games;
- paying her respects at important monuments including the Holodomor Memorial Monument in honour of the millions of Ukrainians who died of starvation during the Soviet famine of 1932–1933 and the Chernobyl Museum to meet with Canadians and Ukrainians who were instrumental in organizing and implementing relief efforts following the disaster;
- visiting important landmarks such as the Kyiv-Pechersk Lavra in Kyiv, a historic Orthodox Christian Monastery recognized as a UNESCO World Heritage Site; and
- hosting an Art Matters forum to explore current Canadian–Norwegian approaches to arts bridging geographic and cultural distances.

Chapter Twelve

THE HEIR TO THE THRONE

This is, I believe, what the Crown is all about — helping to emphasize the emotional bond between individual citizens and the ideals, values, and traditions the country holds dear. It is a privilege and a challenge to fulfill to the best of my ability the unique trust placed in me as Heir to the Throne of the Crown in Canada.
— Prince Charles' foreword to *Saskatchewan Royal Reflections*, detailing his 2001 tour of the province.

When announcing the Royal tour of Saskatchewan by Prince Charles in 2001, provincial secretary Pat Lorje characterized the heir to the throne as one of the symbols of Canadian identity. Since Canada is a constitutional monarchy, the heir to the throne is tremendously important, but like the other fifteen countries in the world that will someday call him King, Canada has no official role for Prince Charles. Not mentioned in the constitution, the heir to the throne is allowed much flexibility before they become the Sovereign. Since his birth in 1948, Canadians have learned much about the personality and interests of Prince Charles throughout his tours of every province and territory.

While in Toronto in 2009, Prince Charles toured the Evergreen Brick Works Farmer's Market in the Don Valley.
Department of Canadian Heritage.

THE HEIR TO THE THRONE AND CANADA

Heirs to the throne represent the future of the Crown, and Canada has a long tradition of getting to know their future Sovereigns (and vice versa) since Prince William (the future King William IV) toured the Halifax and Quebec regions in 1786–1787 (the first member of the Royal family to spent time in the country). In fact, every monarch since Confederation has spent time in Canada before ascending the throne:

- Prince Albert Edward (the future King Edward VII) undertook an

The Duke of Cambridge's Personal Canadian Flag flies over Rotary Challenger Park in Calgary, Alberta, during his and the Duchess's official departure ceremony in 2011. The flag is based on the Queen's Personal Canadian Flag, only the centre features the Duke's cypher, composed of the letter W with a coronet above it, which indicates that he is the child of the heir apparent of the Sovereign. Near the top of the flag is the personal three-point white label charged with a red shell (an allusion to his mother Diana, Princess of Wales, whose arms included them). © *Press Association.*

extensive tour of Newfoundland, Nova Scotia, New Brunswick, Prince Edward Island, and the Province of Canada in 1860. The Royal tour included the opening of Montreal's Victoria Bridge, laying the cornerstone of the Parliament Buildings in Ottawa, and meeting with veterans of the War of 1812.

During his visit to the Niagara Peninsula, the Prince met eighty-five-year-old Laura Secord, learning about her heroic actions during the American invasion of 1813 (unrecognized by the Canadian government). After returning to England, Prince Albert Edward sent Secord £85 — the only financial compensation and recognition she ever received.

- Prince George and Princess Mary (the future King George V and Queen Mary) travelled from coast to coast in 1901 as Duke and Duchess of Cornwall and York. During this tour, the Prince recorded that he had shook the hands of 24,855 people, received 544 addresses, laid 21 foundation stones, given 100 speeches, and presented 4,329 medals.

The Prince first came to Canada in 1883 to visit his aunt, Princess Louise (wife of Governor General the Marquess of Lorne), and returned unofficially during his various tours with the Royal Navy. After the 1901 tour, Prince George paid an official visit to Quebec City in 1908 to help celebrate the city's three hundredth anniversary.

- Prince Albert (the future King George VI) spent time in Canada during his service in the Royal Navy as a member of the crew of HMS *Cumberland*. The Prince's biographer J.W. Wheeler-Bennett wrote that during the Prince's visit to Halifax "… the size of Canadian lakes and the immense distance which it is possible to cover by water in penetrating into the heart of the country came as a revelation to him. From that moment on he loved Canada and looked forward to a return visit."

- Prince Edward (the future King Edward VIII) undertook a two-month tour of Canada in 1919. During his visit, the Prince was captivated by the Canadian West, purchasing a ranch near Pekisko, Alberta. "In the midst of that majestic countryside I had suddenly been overwhelmed by an

Edward, Prince of Wales, is shown sitting on a bull at his ranch near Pekisko, Alberta, in 1923. He was the only monarch (as King Edward VIII) to own private property in Canada. Glenbow Archives, NA-5652-23.

irresistible longing to immerse myself, if only momentarily, in the simple life of the western prairies," the Prince later wrote. Edward returned to Canada for seven weeks in 1923, which included a visit to his beloved ranch. In 1927 he made his last visit before he became Sovereign, touring the country with his brother, Prince George, to mark the Diamond Jubilee (sixtieth anniversary) of Confederation.

- Princess Elizabeth (the future Queen Elizabeth II) toured Canada for thirty-five days in 1951, becoming the first member of the Royal family to fly across the Atlantic.

During a tour of Canada in 1951, Princess Elizabeth (now Queen Elizabeth II) participated in a square dance at Rideau Hall.
Frank Royal / Library and Archives Canada, PA-154623.

PRINCE CHARLES IN CANADA

At the time of publication, Prince Charles has toured Canada fifteen times since first arriving in 1970. These tours have been diverse in their experiences, exposing the Prince to many different areas of the country:

- The Prince of Wales spent thirty-five days in Canadian waters, including a week in the Northwest Territories in 1975. During this tour, Prince Charles dove under the Arctic ice in Resolute Bay.
- Prince Charles has celebrated unique Canadian events such as the two hundredth anniversary of the arrival of the Loyalists, the Calgary Stampede, Expo '86, The Royal Agricultural Winter Fair, and the signing of various First Nations' treaties.
- In the early 1970s, Prince Charles received his pilot training on helicopters over three weeks while training at CFB (Canadian Forces Base) Gagetown, New Brunswick.

A TWENTY-FIRST-CENTURY PRINCE

Delivering the prestigious *Richard Dimbelby Lecture* in 2009, Prince Charles highlighted areas that he has been passionate about for decades: the built and natural environments, architecture, agriculture, healthcare, and responsible business practices. The Prince's interests in these diverse areas are reflected in his patronages and charities, and have been internationally recognized. The Prince was honoured in 2007 with the 10th Global Environmental Citizen Award by the Harvard Medical School's Center for Health and the Global Environment for his extensive work on behalf of the built and natural environments

Personal Canadian Flag of the Prince of Wales. The flag is similar to the Queen's, but the centre features the badge, commonly known as the Prince of Wales's feathers, used by the heir apparent to the reigning monarch. Near the top of the flag is the traditional heraldic mark of an eldest male child, the three-point white label. Image and description courtesy of the Department of Canadian Heritage.

Prince Charles dives under the Arctic ice at Resolute Bay, Northwest Territories, in 1975.
©*Press Association.*

— areas of great interest to many Canadians. Environmentalist and former American vice-president Al Gore reminded the readers of the *Harvard Gazette* that, "Prince Charles has been a forward thinker on environmental issues since the 1970s, on issues ranging from sustainable agriculture to climate change."

THE PRINCE AND CANADIAN SOCIETY

Whether it is participating with Canadians in the International Day for the Elimination of Racial Discrimination (1998) or awarding the 2009 Prince of Wales Prize for Municipal

Heritage Leadership (created in his honour in 1999) to the City of Edmonton (joining Aurora, Markham, Victoria, Saint John, Quebec City, Perth, Annapolis Royal, and St. John's), Prince Charles has been very involved in issues that concern Canadians.

The Prince is patron of Canadian Business for Social Responsibility (CBSR), which encourages businesses to help solve social problems through such initiatives as *Seeing is Believing* (a program that takes business leaders into communities to see the issues first-hand). During his 2009 tour of the country, the Prince met with around thirty senior chief executive officers (CEOs) to discuss the responsibilities businesses have in Canadian society. The CBSR signed the Copenhagen Communiqué — an important statement from the international business community ahead of the major United Nations Climate Change Conference.

THE PRINCE'S CHARITIES

This international group of not-for-profit organizations work together with the Prince as their president, to raise over $162 million annually. In fact, of the twenty charities that are part of this group, eighteen were personally founded by the Prince. The charities are organized into four broad areas of interest: opportunity and enterprise, the built environment, reasonable business, and education. The Prince's charities not only have branches in Canada, but have lead to the creation of brother and sister charities across the country — an example being the Canadian Youth Business Foundation (modelled after the Prince's Youth Business Trust, which helps disadvantaged youth enter the workforce).

THE DUKE OF CAMBRIDGE

As the eldest son of the Prince of Wales, Prince William (now the Duke of Cambridge) is second-in-line to the Canadian throne. With this in mind, the Duke's presence in Canadian society has seen a sharp increase.

"As a unifying figure who is both inspirational and reassuringly familiar, Prince William seems ideally suited to defend Canada's important tradition of constitutional monarchy against cynics and continue the good work of his grandmother Queen Elizabeth II."— Maclean's *magazine editorializing on the engagement of Prince William to Catherine Middleton — now the Duchess of Cambridge — in 2010. Prince William is currently second in line to the throne.* ©Press Association.

A wedding is a milestone in anyone's family, giving its members a chance to celebrate and take stock of their accomplishments both past and present. Prince William and Catherine Middleton's wedding provided the same opportunity, but on a national level. As Governor General David Johnston explained at the launch of a commemorative stamp of the Royal wedding: "The marriage of Prince William and Miss Middleton is reason to celebrate, because they represent the future of the Crown in Canada."

The subsequent Royal tour of the Duke and Duchess of Cambridge was a tremendous success, with the couple focusing media attention on many different aspects of the country and connecting with a wide cross-section of the population (especially the youth). Their 2011 visit came on the heels of a 2010 tour of the Queen and Duke of Edinburgh and a 2009 tour of the Prince of Wales and Duchess of Cornwall, highlighting three senior generations of the Royal family working in Canada.

Chapter Thirteen

THE COMMONWEALTH AND THE QUEEN'S OTHER REALMS

As well as being Queen of Canada, Elizabeth II is also Sovereign of fifteen other independent states, as well as Head of the Commonwealth (an organization of which Canada is a senior member).

THE COMMONWEALTH OF NATIONS

The modern Commonwealth evolved out of the old British Empire during the twentieth century, especially after the Statute of Westminster (1931) and the 1949 London Declaration that stated all members would be "voluntarily and freely associated." Today, fifty-four states make up this organization encompassing over two billion of the planet's inhabitants. Traditionally, member states were former territories within the British Empire, but the Commonwealth has evolved to include states will no such relationship. The Commonwealth Secretariat, based in London (UK), affirms:

> Commonwealth countries work together in a spirit of co-operation, partnership and understanding. This openness and flexibility are

"I address you today as Queen of sixteen United Nations Member States and as Head of the Commonwealth of fifty-four countries." Queen Elizabeth II addresses the United Nations General Assembly, on Tuesday, July 6, 2010, at the United Nations headquarters in New York. ©Press Association.

integral to the Commonwealth's effectiveness. Emphasis on equality has helped it play leading roles in decolonisation, combating racism and advancing sustainable development in poor countries ... The Commonwealth is part of the world that it serves, sharing the same interests as those of its citizens: democratic freedom and economic and social development.

Members of the Commonwealth and the year they entered (*names with an asterisk were never part of the British Empire):

Antigua and Barbuda (1981)
Australia (1931)
Bahamas (1973)

Bangladesh (1972)

Barbados (1966)

Belize (1981)

Botswana (1966)

Brunei (1984)

Cameroon (1995)

Canada (1931)

Cyprus (1961)

Dominica (1978)

Fiji (1970 — expelled in 2006)

Gambia (1965)

Ghana (1957)

Grenada (1974)

Guyana (1966)

India (1947)

Ireland (1931 — withdrew in 1949)

Jamaica (1962)

Kenya (1963)

Kiribati (1979)

Lesotho (1966)

Malawi (1964)

Malaysia (1963)

Maldives (1982)

Malta (1964)

Mauritius (1968)

*Mozambique (1995)

Namibia (1990)

Nauru (1968)

New Zealand (1931)

Nigeria (1960)

Pakistan (1947)

Papua New Guinea (1975)
*Rwanda (2009)
Saint Kitts and Nevis (1983)
Saint Lucia (1979)
Saint Vincent and the Grenadines (1979)
Samoa (1970)
Seychelles (1976)
Sierra Leone (1961)
Singapore (1965)
Solomon Islands (1978)
South Africa (1931)
Sri Lanka (1948)
Swaziland (1968)
Tanzania (1964)
Tonga (1970)
Trinidad and Tobago (1962)
Tuvalu (1978)
Uganda (1962)
United Kingdom (1931)
Vanuatu (1980)
Zambia (1964)
Zimbabwe (1980 — suspended in 2002, withdrew in 2003)

———————

HEAD OF THE COMMONWEALTH

It was the 1949 London Declaration that affirmed King George VI as a symbol of the free association of its members. This affirmation meant that members of the Commonwealth did not have to recognize the King as Sovereign, allowing states that choose the republican form of government (as in the case of India) to remain a part of the organization. Today there are more republics in the Commonwealth than any other form of government.

When her father died in 1952, Elizabeth II became Head of the Commonwealth, but it is important to note that the role of the Crown in relation to the Commonwealth is changing, as its website explains "... when the Queen dies or if she abdicates, her heir will not automatically become Head of the Commonwealth. It will be up to the Commonwealth heads of government to decide what they want to do about this symbolic role."

As Head of the Commonwealth, the Queen holds discussions with its leaders (in individual audiences or larger functions), visits the host country of each summit, delivers a Commonwealth Day broadcast, and is present at other Commonwealth Day events. Largely thanks to the passion of the Queen, the role of Head of the Commonwealth continues to develop along with the organization it represents.

HIGH COMMISSIONERS

To distinguish fellow members of the Commonwealth, their senior diplomats in Canada are called high commissioners instead of ambassadors. Rather than an embassy, a Commonwealth state establishes a High Commission to represent its government to Canada (as Canada does in other Commonwealth countries).

Left: The Queen's Personal Flag for Australia.

Right: The Queen's Personal Flag for Barbados.

Top Left: The Queen's Personal Flag for Jamaica.

Top Right: The Queen's Personal Flag for New Zealand.

Bottom: The Queen's Personal Flag for the United Kingdom.

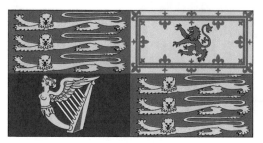

THE QUEEN'S OTHER REALMS

As well as being Queen of Canada, Elizabeth II is also recognized independently as Sovereign of fifteen other states around the world. These are called Commonwealth Realms. The Queen's title and position within each Commonwealth Realm is unique to each specific country. For example, laws are made in the name of the Queen of Papua New Guinea for that country, and when the Queen is acting in her role as Sovereign of that state, she does so independent from her role as Queen of Canada. It is because the Queen embodies each state individually, and not the political views of their governments, that she is able to fulfill her duties as Queen of Canada without conflicting with any of those of her other Commonwealth Realms. The Crown is an institution that has grown to become specific to the country in which it now finds itself planted. No longer just a British monarchy, the Crown is separately a Jamaican monarchy, Tuvaluan monarchy, Canadian monarchy, et cetera.

Currently, Elizabeth II is recognized as Queen of the following Commonwealth Realms: Antigua and Barbuda, Australia, The Bahamas, Barbados, Belize, Canada, Grenada, Jamaica, New Zealand, Papua New Guinea, St. Christopher and Nevis, St. Lucia, St. Vincent and the Grenadines, Solomon Islands, Tuvalu, and the United Kingdom of Great Britain and Northern Ireland.

NO TWO GOVERNORS GENERAL ARE ALIKE

Even though the Queen has sixteen governors general representing her around the world (as well as lieutenant governors and governors), each and every one of them has a different perspective on Walter Bagehot's "rights," as well as different relationships with their governments. The role of the governor general of Australia is very different from that of Canada, because the office has evolved to meet the needs of its country.

DID YOU KNOW?

- The Queen made her first televised Christmas address in 1957, sent her first email in 1976, launched her official website in 1997, joined YouTube in 2007, started "tweeting" in 2009, and became a member of Facebook in 2010. The Queen also owns her own BlackBerry.
- The Queen made her first live television address in on July 1, 1957, for Dominion Day (Canada Day) while she was in the country.
- The Honourable Lincoln M. Alexander became the first member of the African-Canadian community to serve as a representative of the Queen of Canada when he was appointed lieutenant governor of Ontario in 1985 and served until 1991. Before representing the Crown, Mr. Alexander had been the first black Member of Parliament. He was elected in 1968, becoming Minister of Labour in 1979. Hamilton's Lincoln Alexander Parkway is named after its favourite son (declared the "greatest Hamiltonian of all time" in 2006), even though the former lieutenant governor has never had a driver's license!
- The first Commonwealth Games were held in Hamilton, Ontario, in 1930.
- The Honourable Dr. Stephen Worobetz became the first Ukrainian-Canadian to be appointed to the position of lieutenant governor of Saskatchewan in 1977.

- Prince Harry, the Queen's grandson, spent thirty-three days training at CFB (Canadian Forces Base) Suffield, Alberta, in 2008.
- Even though representative and responsible government first emerged in Nova Scotia, the Legislative Assembly did not have a mace until 1928 (a gift from former Chief Justice Robert E. Harris and Mrs. Harris).
- The oldest organized sporting event in North America is the Royal St. John's Regatta on Quidi Vidi Lake in Newfoundland. Stretching back to the 1700s, the regatta has always maintained a strong relationship with the Sovereign, including visits by Prince Albert Edward in 1860 and Queen Elizabeth II in 1978, as well as continued patronage by the province's lieutenant governors. The event was given its "Royal" designation by the Queen in 1993.
- The Canadian Victoria Cross contains a mixture of several types of metals: the gun metal used in the production of the British Victoria Crosses (captured cannons from the Crimean War), metal from an 1867 Confederation Medal, as well as elements from all regions of Canada.
- Queen Elizabeth II is the first monarch in our history to celebrate a sixtieth wedding anniversary (her wedding to Prince Philip was on November 20, 1947).
- The Queen's signature is "Elizabeth R," the "R" standing for "Regina" (meaning *Queen* in Latin).
- There are six golf courses in Canada that have permission to use the "Royal" prefix: Royal Colwood Golf Club (British Columbia), Royal Mayfair Golf Club (Alberta), Royal Montreal Golf Club (Quebec), Royal Ottawa Golf Club (Ontario), Royal Quebec Golf Club (Quebec), and the Royal Regina Golf Club (Saskatchewan).
- Although the national golfing body rebranded itself as Golf Canada in 2010, the organization is still legally registered as the Royal Canadian Golf Association (founded in 1895 and granted permission to use the "Royal" prefix by Queen Victoria in 1896).
- The oldest educational institution in Canada is Université Laval, which was founded with the permission of King Louis XIV as a seminary by Monseigneur François de Laval, the first Bishop of New France. Located in Quebec City, the institution was granted a Royal charter by Queen Victoria in 1852.

New Westminster Mayor Wayne Wright sets off one of the twenty-one anvil shots that make up the Ancient and Honourable Hyack Anvil Battery Salute, May 19, 2008. Photo by Tony Fox.

- Canada's (and indeed the Commonwealth's, excluding the United Kingdom) oldest chartered English-speaking university is the University of King's College in Nova Scotia, which began in New York by Royal Charter granted by King George II in 1756. In 1802, after the American Revolution, Loyalists re-established the university in Nova Scotia (the American campus would eventually be reorganized as Columbia University).

- Every year, the Gatineau Historical Society organizes a memorial to Private Richard Rowland Thompson, who is buried at Chelsea Pioneer Cemetery. Private Thompson received one of eight scarves hand-knitted by Queen Victoria for his act of kindness during the Anglo-Boer War. Saving a severely injured man who had been shot in the throat at Paardeberg, Private Thompson was an example of the heroism shown by young men in the Queen's forces.

- In 2002, frustrated Member of Parliament Keith Martin tried to remove the mace from the House of Commons. The Speaker found Mr. Martin in contempt of Parliament, and he was ordered to apologize before he could return to his seat in the House.

- The first Secretary-General of the Commonwealth was Canadian Arnold Smith in 1965.

- In New Westminster, British Columbia, the Queen's birthday (a.k.a. Victoria Day) is celebrated with a twenty-one-anvil salute at Queen's Park Stadium. The community once had the traditional twenty-one-cannon salute, until the military left (taking the cannons with them), and the honour was taken up by the local Volunteer Fire Department.

- In 1959, the Queen met members of the Inuit community in Stratford, Ontario. This was the first meeting in history between the Royal family and the Inuit.

- The practice of having a Christmas tree became widespread in Canada after Queen Victoria's husband, Prince Albert, popularized the practice. An image of the Royal family around a Christmas tree (originally published in an 1848 edition of the *London Illustrated* News) was published in the United States magazine *Godey's Lady's Book* in 1850, which led to the custom being adopted by many Canadian and American families.

- The Right Honourable Vincent Massey, governor general of Canada from 1952 until 1959, was to become the first knight of the Most Noble Order of the Garter (England's most ancient order, founded in 1348) who was not from the United Kingdom. The Canadian government did not support the appointment (citing that it went against a long policy of not allowing citizens to be given titles), and the Queen instead presented Massey with the prestigious Royal Victorian Chain.

- The Honourable Dr. Sylvia Fedoruk was not only the first female lieutenant governor of Saskatchewan (1988–1994), she was also involved in the development of the world's first Cobalt 60 unit used in the treatment of cancer, as well as one of the first nuclear medicine scanning machines. A professor of oncology and associate member in physics at the University of Saskatchewan, Dr. Fedoruk became the first female member of the Atomic Energy Control Board of Canada in 1973. As an athlete, Dr. Fedoruk held the 1947 Canadian record for women's javelin and was a member of the 1961 Canadian ladies' curling championship team.
- Every year since 1970, the lieutenant governor and chief justice of Saskatchewan co-chair a prayer breakfast attended by over seven hundred people.
- The Salish First Nation conferred the title "Mother of all People" on Queen Elizabeth II in 1959.
- Sir Samuel Leonard Tilley (the man credited with coming up with the name "Dominion" of Canada) twice served as lieutenant governor of New Brunswick (1873–1878 and 1885–1893).
- In 1992, the Canadian Heraldic Authority created a baton for the Speaker of the House of Commons. Inscribed along the base of the baton are the words *pro regina et patria* ("For Queen and Country").
- Early Quebec church architecture is called Louis XIV style.
- The Canadian Crown recognizes one title from New France: the Baron de Longueuil. Originally granted by King Louis XIV to Charles le Moyne de Longueuil in 1700, the current holder is Dr. Michael Grant, 12th Baron de Longueuil, who resides in England.

Barons de Longeuil:
- Charles II le Moyne, 1st Baron de Longueuil (1700–1729)
- Charles III le Moyne, 2nd Baron de Longueuil (1729–1755)
- Charles-Jacques le Moyne, 3rd Baron de Longueuil (1755)
- Marie-Charles le Moyne, 4th Baroness de Longueuil (1755–1841)

- Charles William Grant, 5th Baron de Longueuil (1841–1848)
- Charles James Irwin Grant, 6th Baron de Longueuil (1848–1879)
- Charles Colmore Grant, 7th Baron de Longueuil (1879–1898)
- Reginald Charles Grant, 8th Baron de Longueuil (1898–1931)
- John Charles Moore Grant, 9th Baron de Longueuil (1931–1938)
- Ronald Charles Grant, 10th Baron de Longueuil (1938–1959)
- Raymond Grant, 11th Baron de Longueuil (1959–2004)
- Michael Grant, 12th Baron de Longueuil (2004–present day)

• The Crown, in consultation with the Canadian government, has granted hereditary titles (peerages) to Canadians for service to the country. These titles are:

- Baron Mount Stephen — Baronet (1886), Baron (1891) — (extinct)
- Baroness Macdonald of Earnscliffe (1891) (wife of Sir John A. Macdonald) (extinct)
- Baron Strathcona and Mount Royal (1897). The current holder is Donald Euan Howard, 4th Baron Strathcona and Mount Royal (former British politician)
- Baron Shaughnessy (1916). The current holder is Charles Shaughnessy, 5th Baron Shaughnessy (a British actor)
- Baron Atholstan (1917) — (extinct)

• The British Crown (separate from the Canadian) has granted titles (peerages) to Canadians, without consulting the Canadian government, for service to Britain, the Empire, and later the Commonwealth:

- Baron Haliburton (1898) — (extinct)
- Viscount Pirrie — Baron (1906), Viscount (1921) — (extinct)
- Baron Beaverbrook — Baronet (1916), Baron (1917). The current holder is Maxwell Aitken, 3rd Baron Beaverbrook
- Baron Morris (1918). The current holder is Michael Morris, 3rd Baron Morris.
- Viscount Bennett (1941) — (extinct)
- Baron Thomson of Fleet (1964). The current holder is David Thomson, 3rd Baron Thomson
- Baron Black of Crossharbour (2001), life peerage to Conrad Black

- On September 10, 1621, King James VI (of Scotland) and I (of England) signed a grant to Sir William Alexander covering all of the lands "... between our Colonies of New England and Newfoundland, to be known as New Scotland [or *Nova Scotia* in Latin], making the territory an extension of mainland Scotland. At the suggestion of Sir William Alexander, King James announced his intention to create a new order of baronets to encourage settlement of the fledgling colony of Nova Scotia. The plan was implemented in 1625 by King Charles I, and part of Edinburgh Castle was declared Nova Scotian territory so that baronets could be officially installed "within" the colony for a fee paid to the Crown and Alexander. A hereditary title that still exists, the baronets of Nova Scotia enjoy the privilege of wearing the arms of Nova Scotia as a badge, are addressed as Sir, and place Bt. or Bart. after their names.

  Harsh weather made settlement in Nova Scotia difficult, and the Scottish colony's fate was sealed when King Charles I returned the region to France with the signing of the Treaty of Suza in 1629. Still, the loss of Nova Scotia did not end the baronetcies, and their descendants still bear the titles granted nearly four hundred years ago. It is important to note that baronetcies are not a Canadian honour (rather they flowed from the Scottish Crown that is now included within that of the United Kingdom), and few baronets actually live in Canada. Still, their impact on the settlement and development of Nova Scotia is worth noting.

  A monument exists in Halifax to commemorate Sir Willliam Alexander, which reads:

His efforts to create a New
Scotland in the New World
led to the Royal Charter of
Nova Scotia, 1621
Attempts at settlement 1622–3
The creating of the Order
of Knight Baronets of

Nova Scotia 1624–5
The Coat-of-Arms of
Nova Scotia, 1626
and the occupation of
Port Royal
by Scottish settlers, 1629–32

In 1987, the Canadian Coast Guard launched the CCGS *Sir William Alexander* in the colonizer's honour.

- The first Royal visitor to Canada ended up becoming one of its Kings! Prince William (the future William IV) commanded HMS *Pegasus*, visiting Newfoundland and Halifax in 1786. The following year the prince travelled by canoe and horseback as far west as Cornwall, using the various waterways of Upper and Lower Canada. The Prince celebrated his twenty-first birthday off the coast of Newfoundland and Labrador.

- The origin of the firing of the twenty-one-gun salute, or Royal Salute, is largely unknown. Superstition holds that salutes must always be given in odd numbers. Gun salutes in Canada are given to royalty, nations, and individuals.

- Toasts to the Queen and other members of the Royal family should always be made with water unless you are aboard one of Her Majesty's Canadian Ships. Toasting with water while at sea carries with it the superstition that the person being toasted will drown. The Canadian Navy also maintains the tradition of remaining seated while toasting the Queen's health.

- When Walter Paterson arrived on St. John's Island (now called Prince Edward Island) in 1770 as the colony's first governor, the island's population numbered only three hundred people.

- The Honourable Sir William P. Howland, lieutenant governor of Ontario (1868–73), was the only American-born Father of Confederation.

- The Honourable George Stanley served as lieutenant governor of New Brunswick from 1982 until 1987. Stanley is credited with suggesting the final design for the Canadian national flag in 1964.

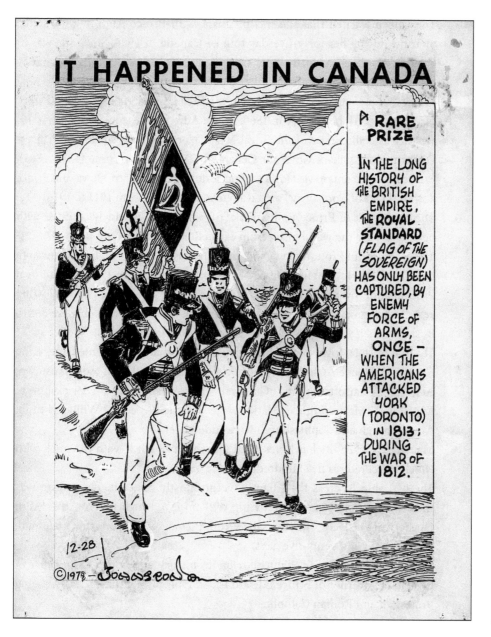

Throughout the history of Canada and the Commonwealth, the Royal Standard (flag of the Sovereign) has only been captured once: when the Americans attacked York (Toronto) in 1813 during the War of 1812. This illustration was produced in 1978 by Gordon Johnston.

With permission of Mairead Johnston-Spooner.

- The Queen learned that she was pregnant with Prince Andrew (The Duke of York) during her forty-five-day tour of Canada in 1959. Since she was in Canada, the Queen informed her Canadian prime minister of the pregnancy before his British counterpart.
- Five of Queen Victoria's children lived in or visited Canada: Albert Edward (Prince of Wales) toured the country in 1860, Prince Alfred made stops in Halifax in his capacity as commander of the Royal Navy's North Atlantic squadron, Princess Louise was the wife of Governor General the Marquess of Lorne (1878–1883), Prince Leopold came to visit Princess Louise during her time in Ottawa, and Prince Arthur (Duke of Connaught) served as governor general from 1911 to 1916.
- The hard work of Prince Philip, Duke of Edinburgh, is widely credited with helping to save the wood bison from extinction.
- The oldest site of Protestant worship in Canada is St. Paul's Anglican Church (a National Historic Site) in Halifax, Nova Scotia. Founded in 1749 after a Royal Proclamation by King George II, the church was constructed the following year. The original timbers used in the construction of the church were cut in Boston (which was still loyal to the Crown at the time).
- The first thirteen townships surveyed in Upper Canada were named after King George III, Queen Charlotte, and eleven of their children: Adolphustown, Augusta, Charlottenburgh, Cornwall, Edwardsburgh, Fredericksburgh, Kingston, Marysburgh, Matilda, Osnabruck, and Williamsburgh. Ameliasburgh and Sophiasburgh were added later.
- Maurice "Rocket" Richard presented Queen Elizabeth II with the puck with which he scored his five hundredth goal in 1959.
- The first ship to cross the Atlantic Ocean mostly under its own steam was the *Royal William* (named after King William IV), which was constructed in Quebec City in 1831. The ship sailed from Pictou, Nova Scotia, to Gravesend, Great Britain, in twenty-five days.
- Highlighting the island's colourful religious history, appointees to the office of lieutenant governor of Prince Edward Island typically alternate between being Protestant and Roman Catholic.

- The Victorian Order of Nurses was organized in 1897 as a gift to commemorate Queen Victoria's Diamond Jubilee (sixtieth anniversary of ascending the throne).
- Crown Royal Whisky was created in 1939 by Seagram's to mark the Royal tour of King George VI and Queen Elizabeth.
- Sir John Thompson, prime minister of Canada (1892–94), died while sitting at Queen Victoria's dinner table in Windsor Castle.
- Parliament Hill's Queen's Gates face Wellington Street and are only opened for the arrival of the Sovereign or their representative.
- One of the few hereditary honours that remain in North America is held by the descendants of the Loyalists who fled the Thirteen Colonies to settle in what would become Canada. In order to recognize their loyalty, Lord Dorchester (governor of Quebec in 1789) declared that, "Those Loyalists who have adhered to the Unity of the Empire, and joined the Royal Standard before the Treaty of Separation in the year 1783 [the year the United Kingdom recognized the independence of the United States], and all their Children and their Descendants by either sex, are to be distinguished by the following Capitals, affixed to their names: U.E. Alluding to their great principle The Unity of the Empire." Today thousands of Canadians write these initials after their name.
- Governor General Adrienne Clarkson (1999–2005) was inducted into the Kainai Chieftainship of the Blood Tribe of southwestern Alberta with the name "Grandmother of Many Nations."
- Vancouver Island's Governor James Douglas presided over North America's smallest legislature when it was opened in 1856. Forty voters elected seven members.
- Prince Arthur, Queen Victoria's third son and future Duke of Connaught, was given the Fenian Medal for his participation as a captain with the Montreal detachment of the Rifle Brigade during the 1870 Fenian Raids.
- La Citadelle, the governor general's second official residence, was the site of the Quebec Conferences of 1943 and 1944. Hosted by Governor General the Earl of Athlone, world leaders Winston Churchill, Franklin D. Roosevelt, and William Lyon MacKenzie King devised D-Day during these meetings.

- One of the sons of Benedict Arnold, the American traitor of the Revolutionary War, was appointed as aide-de-camp to King William IV.
- Sir Arthur Currie (commander of the Canadian Corps) was knighted on the battlefield by King George V after the capture of Vimy Ridge.
- The clergy at St. Mark's Church in Port Hope, Ontario, have permission from Queen Elizabeth II to wear scarlet cassocks. Traditionally, Anglican clergy may wear red in any church that the Sovereign has attended.
- For the coronation of Queen Victoria, a general amnesty was granted to the rebels responsible for the Lower Canadian Rebellion of 1837 (including George-Étienne Cartier).
- The oldest road in Ontario was ordered cut by Lieutenant Governor John Graves Simcoe in 1793. Named Dundas Street after Henry Dundas (secretary of state for the Home Department and fellow abolitionist), the section passing through the Town of Dundas is called Governor's Road in Simcoe's honour.
- The Honourable Steven L. Point was appointed as British Columbia's first Aboriginal person (of the Stó:lō First Nation) to serve as Queen's Representative in 2007. His Honour is also identified by British Columbia's Government House as Xwĕ lī qwĕl tĕl, which translates from the Halq'eméylem dialect of Halkomelem to mean "Great Speaker."
- There are only two legislatures in the Commonwealth in which the government sits to the left of the Speaker: Prince Edward Island and Newfoundland and Labrador. The explanation given for both legislatures is that it was warmer on the left side of the buildings due to the sun, those seats were coveted by the government in the winter.
- The principal chief of southwestern Alberta's Blood Tribe was Red Crow (1830–1900), who led his people through their negotiations with the Canadian government. As a sign of honour and respect, Prince Edward (1919) and Prince Charles (1977) were also given the name "Red Crow" by the Blood Tribe.
- Phillips Callbeck, the acting governor of Prince Edward Island (then called St. John's Island), was kidnapped along with the Great Silver Seal (the Great Seal of the colony) by American privateers in 1775. The seal was never recovered,

Hatley Castle, British Columbia. The castle was built in 1908 by James Dunsmuir while he was lieutenant governor of the province (1906–09). Hatley was also known as HMCS (His Majesty's Canadian Ship) Royal Roads — an officer training establishment from 1940–42. By 1942, the building became the home of the Royal Canadian Naval College (the predecessor of the Royal Roads Military College that existed from 1968 until 1995). Today, Hatley Castle is known as part of the Royal Roads University. Photo by Brandon Godfrey.

and was most likely melted down by George Washington's revolutionary army. Callbeck was eventually returned.

- Canada had a long tradition of using Royal trains (trains set aside for the exclusive use of members of the Royal family and their entourage) before the practicality of air travel gained favour. The first member of the Royal family to make use of a Royal train was Prince Albert Edward (the future King Edward VII) during his 1860 Royal tour. The famous 1901 tour by Prince George and Princess Mary (the Duke and Duchess of Cornwall and York, as well as the future King George V and Queen Mary) was the first Royal train to travel coast to coast. The most famous Royal train was the one used by King George VI and Queen Elizabeth during their historic forty-four-day tour of Canada in 1939. Before becoming Queen, Princess Elizabeth used a Royal train during her 1951 tour of Canada with her husband Prince Philip.

- When she was appointed in 1990, Prince Edward Islander the Honourable Marion Reid became the first female lieutenant governor in the Maritimes. Ms. Reid was also the first female Speaker of the PEI Legislative Assembly, as well as the first Catholic to be elected in her constituency of 1st Queens.
- The Crown Jewels were sent to Canada for safekeeping during the Second World War. It was also proposed that King George VI, his wife Queen Elizabeth, and their daughters, Princesses Elizabeth (now the Queen) and Margaret, would relocate to Canada. In preparation for their move, Hatley Castle in Colwood, British Columbia, was purchased as a residence for the family. The Royal family declined to leave the United Kingdom during the war years, and indeed the King insisted on staying in London throughout the blitz.
- Manitoba Lieutenant Governor the Honourable James Duncan McGregor (in office 1929–1934) was the first farmer to cultivate alfalfa in Western Canada.
- Governor General the Marquess of Lorne was the first representative of the Queen to visit the Northwest Territory in 1881. It was the governor general who had the government name part of the region Alberta after his wife, Princess Louise Caroline Alberta.
- The first member of the Royal family to enter the United States was the Duke of Kent in 1793. The Duke did so by crossing the frozen St. Lawrence River from Quebec.
- There is a movement to have former Governor General Georges Vanier and his wife Pauline declared saints by the Roman Catholic Church. Their devotion to service and family was so strong that there is hope by many that they will be jointly declared saints, highlighting their strong and loving marriage. Many people see Georges Vanier and his predecessor Vincent Massey as exemplars of what governors general should be.
- The Duke of Kent was commander-in-chief of the King's forces in North America from 1799 to 1802. This appointment was coveted by Prince Edward, since he aspired to become governor general, a position that he would never fill.

- Peter Milliken, former Speaker of the House of Commons, is a United Empire Loyalist and uses the post-nominals "UE."
- Canada's national "maple leaf" flag was proclaimed by Queen Elizabeth II in 1965.

- King George V proclaimed his Royal Arms in right of Canada (a.k.a. the Canadian Coat of Arms) in 1921. There was some confusion over Canada's official colours (or tinctures), which some interpreted as green and white. It was not until the creation of the Queen's Personal Flag for Canada in 1961 that red and white was firmly established as the national colours. The rationale for these colours was articulated by an unnamed member of the Arm's Committee (1919–1921):

  The colours of the shield [of the coat of arms] will become the national colours of the dominion ... National sentiment probably is most attached to the maple leaf in its autumnal colouring ... the red maple leaf has been used in service flags to denote men who have sacrificed their lives for the country and Empire. At the present juncture the choice of this emblem, with this touching reminiscence, probably would evoke widespread approval ... The case for white is that it contains an allusion to snow which is characteristic of our climate and our landscape in certain seasons....

- Many Canadians bought their first televisions in 1953 to watch the coronation of Queen Elizabeth II. To ensure that Canadians saw the coronation the same day as the British, the CBC (Canadian Broadcasting Corporation) enlisted the help of the Royal Canadian Air Force to fly the footage across the Atlantic. The mission, code-named "Operation Pony Express," was a success.
- Albertan Lieutenant Governor The Honourable J. Percy Page (in office 1959–1966) was the organizer and coach of the Edmonton Grads Women's Basketball Team. From 1914 to 1940, the team won 502 of their 522 games, including four Olympic meets: Paris (1924), Amsterdam (1928), Los Angeles (1932), and Berlin (1936).
- In 1930, it looked like the Duke of York (the future George VI) would be appointed governor general of Canada (at the instigation of Canadian Prime

Road sign for Louis X's Chemin du Roy, Quebec. The Grand Council of New France decreed that a road be constructed in 1706. However, the project was not completed until 1737.

Minister R.B. Bennett). However, King George V was advised not to make such an appointment by the British Secretary of State for the Dominions for fear of offending the Americans by having a member of the Royal family so close to the United States.

- Before being appointed lieutenant governor of Upper Canada, John Graves Simcoe commanded the Queen's Rangers (1st American Regiment) during the American Revolutionary War. The Queen's Rangers wore green tunics, becoming the first European soldiers to use camouflage.

- Princess Louise was the first female member of the Royal family to cross the Atlantic Ocean, when she travelled to Canada after her husband (the Marquess of Lorne) was appointed governor general in 1878.

- The "Fountain of Hope" outside of Rideau Hall was given by the Canadian Football League during the International Year for Disabled Persons in memory of Terry Fox.

- The first Aboriginal person to be appointed as Queen's representative of a Canadian province was Alberta's Honourable Ralph G. Steinhauer (in office 1974–1979).

- The oldest roadway in Canada is The King's Road (Chemin du Roy) linking Montreal, Trois-Rivières, and Quebec City. Built in 1737, the roadway is named after King Louis XV.

- Camilla, Duchess of Cornwall (and wife of the Prince of Wales), is the great-great-granddaughter of Sir Allan MacNab (premier of Canada West and builder of Hamilton's Dundurn Castle).

- Elizabeth II was proclaimed Queen at Ottawa on February 6, 1952, before any of her other realms.

- In 1878, Sir John A. Macdonald (prime minister of Canada) did not show up to meet the newly appointed governor general, the Marquess of Lorne and his wife Princess Louise, due to an alcohol binge.

- During the Labour Day weekend of 1919, Edward, Prince of Wales, raised a specially designed Victory Lone Flag over the Parliament Buildings in Ottawa. The flag was part of a larger campaign to reward the communities that raised

Camilla, Duchess of Cornwall (accompanied by her husband, Prince Charles) views a portrait of one of her ancestors at Dundurn Castle in Hamilton, Ontario, 2009. The Duchess became patron of the Dundurn Castle National Historic Site in 2010. Department of Canadian Heritage.

the most money to help pay for the First World War (1914–1918).

- British Columbia lieutenant governor, the Honourable George Randolph Pearkes (in office 1960–1968), was awarded the Victoria Cross for his skilful handling of his troops during the Battle of Passchendaele. Pearkes was wounded five times during the course of the First World War.

- King François I (1515–1547) personally financed the expedition led by Jacques Cartier in 1534. It was in this French King's name that Cartier claimed New France in April of that year.

- Princess Louise saved the life of her lady-in-waiting during a sleigh accident at Rideau Hall in 1880. Due to slippery conditions, the sleigh started moving too fast, causing the horses to bolt. After toppling on its side, the sleigh was dragged 350 metres, injuring the Princess. Despite having one of her earrings ripped out and muscle damage to her neck and shoulders, Princess Louise held up Eva Langham's head as the sleigh skidded out of control.

- Prince Edward Island is named after Prince Edward, the Duke of Kent, and son of King George III. Edward lived and travelled in Nova Scotia, Upper and Lower Canada throughout 1791 to 1800, making a huge impact in the development of the country. The iconic octagonal town clock in Halifax was designed by the Prince for the inhabitants (known for always being late) in 1803. The Prince was fascinated by octagonal designs and is responsible for numerous buildings across the continent. Prince Edward was also the father of Queen Victoria. Kent Gate in Quebec City was built as a memorial by Queen Victoria to her father in 1879.
- In 1664, Louis XIV (known to history as "The Sun King") laid the foundations of what would become the Quebec Civil Code.
- Ontario's QEW (Queen Elizabeth Way) was named after King George VI's consort (and mother of Queen Elizabeth II), Queen Elizabeth.
- Prince Andrew, the Queen's third child, went on exchange to Lakefield College School in Ontario for six months in 1977.
- King Edward VIII's first appearance overseas was as King of Canada. The King travelled to France to unveil the Vimy Memorial on July 26, 1936.
- Prince Charles has a 9521 km² island named after him in Canada's high Arctic (present-day Nunavut). The island's location was first recorded the same year that the Prince was born (1948).
- When Sir George-Étienne Cartier asked Queen Victoria for permission to name the Victoria Bridge (an engineering feat in its day), the Queen asked how many feet long long it would be. Cartier responded "Your Majesty, when we think of naming something in your honour, it is something that is measured in miles and not in feet."
- It was French King Henri IV who financed the expedition (led by Pierre Dugua, sieur de Mons, and Samuel de Champlain) that saw the founding of the first permanent settlement in Acadia at Île Sainte-Croix in 1608.

The Duke and Duchess of Windsor (formerly King Edward VIII and Wallis Simpson) at EP Ranch near Pekisko, Alberta, in 1941.

Glenbow Archives, NA-4683-1.

- For the 1967 Centennial of Confederation, Queen Elizabeth II presented six pairs of mute (Royal) swans to the City of Ottawa. The descendants of these Royal swans swim the waters of the Rideau River between Carleton University and Cummings Bridge and are protected by the city. One of the pairs was given to Stratford, Ontario, and descendants of the Queen's swans can now be found swimming the Avon River. Stratford's most famous Royal swan was a cob named Clyde, whose grave can be found along the river's banks. Mr. Robert J. Miller (1916–2007) cared for the Stratford swans for almost fifty years, earning the honorary title of "Keeper of the Swans."
- There are only three "Royal" fairs in the world and two of them are in Canada: The Royal Agricultural Winter Fair in Toronto and the Royal Manitoba Winter Fair (the third one is the Royal Agricultural Society of Western Australia).
- King Edward VIII (reigned in 1936) owned a ranch near Pekisko, Alberta. Edward purchased his "EP Ranch" (EP stands for *Edward Princeps*, which is "Prince Edward" in Latin) during his 1919 tour as Prince of Wales. The Prince visited the ranch while he was Prince of Wales, as well as after the abdication crisis (bringing Wallis Simpson with him) as the Duke of Windsor. The ranch was sold in 1962.
- John Graves Simcoe, the first lieutenant governor of Upper Canada, introduced a bill in 1793 that began the process of phasing out slavery. This was the first legislation of its kind in the British Empire.
- The Prince of Wales Trophy (donated by the future Edward VIII in 1924) is presented by the National Hockey League (NHL) to the Eastern Conference playoff champions.
- Ultimately, it was Queen Victoria who chose Ottawa (formally Bytown) as the capital of Canada in 1857. Her son, Albert (the future King Edward VII), laid the cornerstone for the first Parliament Buildings on September 1, 1860. When the centre block of the Parliament Buildings burned down in 1917, Albert's younger brother Prince Arthur (The Duke of Connaught and governor general of Canada) was asked to re-lay the cornerstone.

The only building in the world that displays the Royal cypher (monogram or initials of the Sovereign) of King Edward VIII is Postal Station K in Toronto, Ontario, at 2384 Yonge Street (Montgomery Avenue intersection). Interestingly, the postal outlet is located on the site of Montgomery's Tavern — an important battle of the ill-fated 1837 Upper Canada rebellion. Photo by Jamie Curio.

- Princess Patricia (daughter of the Duke of Connaught, governor general of Canada 1911–1916) loved her time in Canada. During the opening days of the First World War, the princess lent her name to a Canadian army regiment, taking much interest in their training and service. Princess Patricia's Own Canadian Light Infantry has become one of the most famous regiments in Canada and continues its service to this day.
- Prince Edward, Prince of Wales (and future Edward VIII), marched with Canadians into Valenciennes, France, on Armistice Day at the end of the First World War.
- CBC's first broadcast of a 3-D documentary was in 2010 and was called "Queen Elizabeth in 3-D." The production highlighted lost 3-D footage from the 1953 coronation, as well as new sections taken during the 2010 Royal tour.
- The centre block of the Parliament Buildings contains various corbels depicting Canadian Sovereigns since Confederation. The corbel of King Edward VIII is the only instance in the world where the ill-fated monarch is shown wearing a crown (he abdicated in 1936 before his coronation).
- The Queen's Plate (established in 1860) is Canada's oldest thoroughbred race, held each summer at Woodbine Racetrack in Etobicoke, Ontario. The Prince of Wales Stakes (established in 1929) is held annually at the Fort Erie Race Track, although it was originally held at Thorncliffe Park Raceway. Both of these races are part of the Canadian Triple Crown (along with the Breeder's Stakes).
- When the Queen or another member of the Royal family are on board one of the executive planes used by the Canadian government, the aircraft is referred to as the *Royal Flight*.
- During the 1939 Royal tour of King George VI and Queen Elizabeth, Prime Minister William Lyon Mackenzie King remarked in his personal diary that it was "poetic justice" that he would be accompanying the great-grandson of Queen Victoria to the United States, since his grandfather, William Lyon Mackenzie, had been forced to flee to the United States after leading the 1837 Upper Canada Rebellion against the Crown.

The corbel, a piece of stone jutting out of a wall or pillar, depicting a crowned King Edward VIII. © *Senate of Canada.*

- The Duchess of Cambridge's grandfather, Peter Middleton, was stationed at the No. 37 Service Flying Training School near Calgary, Alberta, during the Second World War. A flight instructor with the British Commonwealth Air Training Program, Middleton trained men to be pilots for the Royal Air Force.
- Please check *www.canadiancrown.com*, as new royal information will be posted there as it comes available.

CANADIAN SOVEREIGNS AND THEIR REPRESENTATIVES

FRENCH CROWN

- François I (1524–1547)
- Henri II (1547–1559)
- François II (1559–1560)
- Charles IX (1560–1574)
- Henri III (1574–1589)
- Henri IV (1589–1610)
- Louis XIII (1610–1643)
- Louis XIV (1643–1715)
- Louis XV (1715–1763)

———————

ENGLISH CROWN

- Henry VII (1485–1509)

Her Majesty Queen Victoria. *This portrait hangs in the Senate and has been saved from four separate fires since it was painted by John Partridge (1789–1872) in 1842: twice when Parliament was in Montreal in 1849, once when Parliament was in Quebec City in 1854, and again when the Parliament Buildings burned down in Ottawa in 1916.*
©*Senate of Canada.*

- Henry VIII (1509–1547)
- Edward VI (1547–1553)
- Mary I (1553–1558)
- Elizabeth I (1558–1603)

BRITISH CROWN (ENGLISH, SCOTTISH, AND LATER IRISH)

- James I (1603–1625)
- Charles I (1625–1649)
- Commonwealth period (1649–1660)
- Charles II (1660–1685)
- James II (1685–1688)
- William III (1688–1702) and Mary II (1688–1694)
- Anne (1702–1714)
- George I (1714–1727)
- George II (1727–1760)
- George III (1760–1820)
- George IV (1820–1830)
- William IV (1830–1837)
- Victoria (1837–1848)

CANADIAN CROWN

- Victoria (1849–1901)
- Edward VII (1901–1910)
- George V (1910–1936)
- Edward VIII (1936)

His Majesty King George VI. *Robert Swain, artist, from a portrait by Sir Gerald F. Kelly (1879–1972).* © *Senate of Canada.*

- George VI (1936–1952)
- Elizabeth II (1952–present day)

––––––––––

VICEROYS AND LIEUTENANT GENERALS OF NEW FRANCE

Vice-regal rulers who lived in France and reported directly to the French King. Viceroys governed through a "lieutenant" that until 1636 was usually Samuel de Champlain.

- Aymar de Chaste (1602–1603)
- Pierre Dugua, sieur de Mons (1603–1612). Visited New France from 1604 to 1605, the only viceroy to come to America.
- Charles de Bourbon, comte de Soissons (1612)
- Henri de Bourbon, prince de Condé (1612–1615 and 1619–1620)
- Pons de Lauzières, Marquess de Thémines de Cardillac (1616–1619)
- Henri, duc de Montmorency et de Dampville (1620–1625)
- Henri de Lévis, duc de Ventadour (1625–1626)
- Armand-Jean du Plessis, bishop of Luçon, cardinal of the Roman Catholic Church, duc de Richelieu and de Fronsac, a.k.a. Cardinal Richelieu (1626–1635)

––––––––––

GOVERNORS AND GOVERNORS GENERAL OF CANADA

- Samuel de Champlain (1627–1635)
- Charles de Montmagny (1635–1648)
- Louis d'Ailleboust de Coulonge (1648–1651)
- Jean de Lauzon (1651–1657)
- Le vicomte d'Argenson (1658–1661)
- Le baron d'Avaugour (1661–1663)

- Augustin de Mésy (1663–1665)
- Daniel de Courcelle (1665–1672)
- Le comte de Frontenac (1672–1682 and 1689–1698)
- Joseph-Antoine de La Barre (1682–1685)
- Le marquess de Denonville (1685–1689)
- Hector de Callière (1698–1703)
- Philippe de Vaudreuil (1703–1725)
- Le marquess de Beauharnois (1726–1747)
- Le comte de La Galissonnière (1747–1749)
- Le marquess de La Jonquière (1749–1752)
- Le marquess de Duquesne (1752–1755)
- Pierre de Vaudreuil (1755–1760)
- Jeffrey Amherst (1760–1764)
- James Murray (1764–1768)
- Sir Guy Carleton, Lord Dorchester (1768–1778)
- Frederick Haldimand (1778–1786)
- Sir Guy Carleton, Lord Dorchester (1786–1796)
- Robert Prescott (1796–1807)
- Sir James Craig (1807–1811)
- Sir George Prevost (1812–1815)
- Sir John Sherbrooke (1816–1818)
- The Duke of Richmond (1818–1819)
- The Earl of Dalhousie (1820–1828)
- Lord Aylmer (1830–1835)
- The Earl of Gosford (1835–1838)
- The Earl of Durham (1838)
- Sir John Colborne (1838–1839)
- Lord Sydenham (1839–1841)
- Sir Charles Bagot (1842–1843)
- Lord Metcalfe (1843–1845)
- The Earl of Cathcart (1845–1847)

- The Earl of Elgin (1847–1854)
- Sir Edmund Head (1854–1861)
- Viscount Monck (1861–1868)
- Lord Lisgar (1868–1872)
- The Earl of Dufferin (1872–1878)
- The Marquess of Lorne (1878–1883)
- The Marquess of Lansdowne (1883–1888)
- Lord Stanley of Preston (1888–1893)
- The Earl of Aberdeen (1893–1898)
- The Earl of Minto (1898–1904)
- Earl Grey (1904–1911)
- Prince Arthur, Duke of Connaught (1911–1916)
- The Duke of Devonshire (1916–1921)
- Lord Byng of Vimy (1921–1926)
- Viscount Willingdon of Ratton (1926–1931)
- The Earl of Bessborough (1931–1935)
- Lord Tweedsmuir of Elsfeld (1935–1940)
- The Earl of Athlone (1940–1946)
- Viscount Alexander of Tunis (1946–1952)
- Vincent Massey (1952–1959)
- Georges-Philéas Vanier (1959–1967)
- Roland Michener (1967–1974)
- Jules Léger (1974–1979)
- Edward Schreyer (1979–1984)
- Jeanne Sauvé (1984–1990)
- Ramon John Hnatyshyn (1990–1995)
- Roméo LeBlanc (1995–1999)
- Adrienne Clarkson (1999–2005)
- Michaëlle Jean (2005–2010)
- David Johnston (2010–present day)

Appendix C

OFFICERS AND OFFICIALS OF THE CROWN

AIDE-DE-CAMP

An honorary position, the role of the aide-de-camp varies from province to province. In general, an aide-de-camp is a member of the military, police, or firefighting forces (depending on the province) who attend to the needs of the lieutenant governor during various events throughout their mandate. Sometimes (such as in Alberta) an aide-de-camp is directly involved in the organization and protocol aspects of vice-regal visits, while in other provinces they are only there on the day of the function to attend to the lieutenant governor.

BLACK ROD IN THE SENATE

An ancient office with roots stretching back over six hundred years, "Black Rod" was originally a member of the Sovereign's household before evolving into the personal attendant and messenger of the King/Queen, or their representative, in Parliament. The unusual name comes from the symbol of the office's authority held by the officer: an ebony rod. Parliaments

Mr. Kevin MacLeod
C.V.O., C.D., Usher of
the Black Rod in the
Senate. © *Senate of Canada.*

throughout the Commonwealth employ Black Rods, many of which remain members of the Queen's Household.

From the establishment of Canada's Parliament, there has been an Usher of the Black Rod in Ottawa. Originally called the Gentlemen Usher of the Black Rod in the Senate, the name was altered in 1997 when Mary C. McLaren became the first women to hold the office. Today, Black Rod is in charge of all ceremonial, logistical, and protocol details for events such as the opening of Parliament, state funerals, and the ceremony granting Royal Assent. Greeting dignitaries and running the Senate page program, as well as overseeing the security in the Senate chamber, are also part of Black Rod's responsibilities.

As the personal messenger of the Sovereign, it is the Usher of the Black Rod who enters the House of Commons during the opening of Parliament to summon its members to attend to the Queen, or her representative, in the Senate.

Ushers of the Black Rod in the Senate:

- Kimber, René (1867–1875)
- Kimber, René Edouard (Replaced his father upon his retirement) (1875–1901)
- St. John, Molyneux (1902–1904)
- Chambers, Ernest John (1904–1925)
- Thompson, Andrew Ruthven (1925–1946)
- Lamoureux, Charles Rock (1947–1970)
- Vandelac, A. Guy (1970–1979)
- Bowie, Thomas Guy (1979–1983)
- Askwith, Charles (Acting) (1983–1984)
- Lajoie, Claude G. (1984–1985)
- Jalbert, René M. (1985–1989)
- Gutknecht, Rene (1989–1990)
- Doré, Jean (1990–1997)
- McLaren, Mary C. (1997–2001)
- Armitage, Blair (Acting) (2001–2002)
- Christopher, Terrance J. (2002–2008)
- MacLeod, Kevin (2008–present day)

Sadly, since none of the provinces have retained their upper houses (Quebec was the last province to lose its upper house in 1968) the office of Usher of the Black Rod can only be found in Ottawa. The duties of the provincial Black Rods are now largely exercised by the various sergeants-at-arms — some even carrying an ebony rod during various ceremonies such as the opening of the legislature.

CANADIAN SECRETARY TO THE QUEEN

Charged with organizing and running all aspects of Royal tours by members of the Royal family, this official oversees every detail from the development and planning stages, to the actual events themselves. The Canadian Secretary to the Queen is also charged with drafting any speeches given by the Sovereign as Queen of Canada.

This role is constantly evolving, and the secretary is increasingly being consulted on other matters such as "Royal" designations, patronage applications, and other matters related to Elizabeth II's position as Queen of Canada. The current Canadian Secretary to the Queen is Kevin MacLeod CVO CD.

CANADIAN EQUERRY TO THE QUEEN

Each member of the Royal family has an equerry appointed to them for the duration of a Royal tour. Drawn from the Canadian Forces, the equerry is an officer charged with attending to all requirements of the Queen (or other member of the Royal family) and senior members of her household. The equerry ensures schedules are maintained, and that all necessary protocol is observed. There to ensure that the public enjoy their experience with the Royal family member and that if there are gifts, they are collected for a later presentation. Above all, the equerry's role is to make sure that their charge is comfortable and that their needs are being looked after.

Lieutenant-Commander Scott Nelson (wearing a white naval uniform) attends to the Queen as she inspects a guard of honour on Canada Day, 2010. ©Press Association

The origins of the office stem from the role of a trusted officer of the Sovereign who cared for King's horse after he dismounted. To symbolize the position, equerries wear a decorative gold cord called an *aiguillette* on the right shoulder of their uniform. One story of the origin of the aiguillette is that it was used as a lace to tie together the King's armour when preparing for battle. In addition, equerries wear the cypher of the individual they serve on their epaulettes.

Prior to a Canadian Royal tour, an equerry is appointed, and in the weeks leading up to the tour, takes up residence at Buckingham Palace (or whichever residence of the member of the Royal family they are assigned to) to familiarize themselves with the role and the household. As soon as the member of the Royal family arrives in Canada, the Canadian Equerry becomes the Canadian Equerry-in-Waiting, meaning they are now on duty.

The equerry is also normally the first person to greet the Royal family member in the morning, and the last to bid them good night.

CHATELAINE

Meaning "mistress of a large house," this title traditionally was given to the female spouse of a governor general or lieutenant governor. Only British Columbia, Manitoba, and Nova Scotia continue to use the title.

CHIEF HERALD OF CANADA

The Chief Herald of Canada is responsible for the day-to-day operations of the Canadian Heraldic Authority. The chief herald formally makes every grant of arms to the various petitioners to the authority, with the exception of the governor general, who can exercise this Royal prerogative at their discretion. In 2009, Governor General Michaëlle Jean announced that a heraldic tabard (the traditional garment of heralds) would be created to be worn by the chief herald on special occasions.

Claire Boudreau, Chief Herald of Canada, with her baton and chain of office, 2007. ©Her Majesty in Right of Canada as administered by the Canadian Heraldic Authority 2007.

Mr. Garry Clarke,
sergeant-at-arms of the
Manitoba Legislature.
Photo by Tim Pohl, Government
of Manitoba.

SECRETARIES AND PRIVATE SECRETARIES

Working tirelessly across the country are officials who head the various vice-regal offices and households. For the governor general, this official is called the *Secretary*, while the provinces have *Private Secretaries* (except New Brunswick, which uses the title *Principal Secretary*). It is the (private) secretary who handles the governor general or lieutenant governor's calendar, ensuring that each and every day is organized, efficient, and meets the necessary protocol. These individuals handle the day-to-day running of the office, heading the staff assigned to them (which can vary depending on their jurisdiction). Effectively, a secretary is the right hand of the Queen's representative. In Nova Scotia and British Columbia, the private secretary is also the executive director of their Government Houses (the official residence of the lieutenant governor).

After being elected by his peers in the House of Commons, Peter Milliken is dragged to the Speaker's chair by Prime Minister Paul Martin and leader of the opposition, Stephen Harper, in 2004. © House of Commons.

SERGEANT-AT-ARMS

With roots going as far back as 1279 and King Edward I, the office of sergeant-at-arms has a long history. Charged with protecting the authority of the Speaker, the sergeant-at-arms is the only officer in Parliament (or a provincial legislature) who may handle the mace (itself a symbol of Royal authority). Today, every legislature, as well as the Parliament in Ottawa, has a sergeant-at-arms who is charged with security of the legislature and other property management functions.

SPEAKER

This is an ancient office that emerged from the Middle Ages. The speaker was a spokesperson who represented the common people to the king. The Speaker was the official who presented grievances and petitions to the Sovereign. This was not always the safest job and is the reason why after their election is announced, the new Speaker is dragged to their chair by the prime minister and leader of Her Majesty's official opposition).

Today, the Speaker is the spokesperson and representative for the House of Commons (or provincial legislature) in its dealings with the Crown, Senate, and other bodies outside of Parliament. It is the Speaker's job to ensure the orderly flow of business in the House of Commons, and to ensure that such business observes the rules of the written and unwritten constitution. The Speaker must remain impartial as they maintain order in the House while defending the rights and privileges of its members.

When entering or leaving the House of Commons, the Speaker is preceded by the sergeant-at-arms carrying the mace — the symbol of the authority of the Crown. It is the Speaker who leads the members of the House of Commons into the Senate to attend the Queen or governor general during the opening of Parliament, or a witnessing of Royal Assent.

The Senate also has a Speaker who has similar responsibilities to their counterpart in the House of Commons, but with some differences. Although this is rarely exercised, the Speaker in the Senate is able to participate in debate (although they must leave their chair to do so) and may vote. Charged with maintaining order, the Speaker in the Senate is appointed by the governor general on the recommendation of the prime minister.

TITLES AND FORMS OF ADDRESS

The Sovereign:
Elizabeth the Second, by the Grace of God of the United Kingdom, Canada and Her other Realms and Territories Queen, Head of the Commonwealth, Defender of the Faith
Referred to as: "Your Majesty"; continue with "Ma'am."

The Duke of Edinburgh (Consort to the Queen):
His Royal Highness The Prince Philip, Duke of Edinburgh
Referred to as: "Your Royal Highness"; continue with "Sir."

The Prince of Wales (Prince Charles) and The Duchess of Cornwall (as well as other members of the Royal family):
His Royal Highness The Prince of Wales and Her Royal Highness The Duchess of Cornwall
Referred to as: "Your Royal Highness"; continue with "Sir" or "Ma'am."

The Governor General:
His/Her Excellency, The Right Honourable _____, *Governor General of Canada*
Referred to as "Your Excellency" while in office, and retains "The Right Honourable" for life.

The Royal cypher (monogram or initials of the Sovereign) of King George V appears over the door of the Speaker of the Senate's office. ©Senate of Canada.

The Lieutenant Governor:

His/Her Honour, _____, Lieutenant Governor of _____.

Referred to as "Your Honour" while in office, and "The Honourable" afterward.

WEBSITES

THE QUEEN'S REPRESENTATIVES

Governor General of Canada: *www.gg.ca*
Lieutenant Governor of Alberta: *www.lieutenantgovernor.ab.ca*
Lieutenant Governor of British Columbia: *www.ltgov.bc.ca*
Lieutenant Governor of Manitoba: *www.lg.gov.mb.ca*
Lieutenant Governor of New Brunswick: *www.gnb.ca/lg*
Lieutenant Governor of Newfoundland and Labrador: *www.govhouse.nl.ca*
Lieutenant Governor of Nova Scotia: *www.lieutenant-gouverneur.qc.ca*
Lieutenant Governor of Ontario: *www.lt.gov.on.ca*
Lieutenant Governor of Prince Edward Island: *www.gov.pe.ca/olg*
Lieutenant Governor of Quebec: *www.lieutenant-gouverneur.qc.ca*
Lieutenant Governor of Saskatchewan: *www.ltgov.sk.ca*

———————

The Speaker of the Senate's chair sits in front of the Throne of Canada. ©*Senate of Canada.*

FEDERAL AND PROVINCIAL LEGISLATURES

Parliament of Canada: *www.parl.gc.ca*
Senate of Canada: *www.sen.parl.gc.ca*
Legislative Assembly of Alberta: *www.assembly.ab.ca*
Legislative Assembly of British Columbia: *www.leg.bc.ca*
Legislative Assembly of Manitoba: *www.gov.mb.ca/leg-asmb*
Legislative Assembly of New Brunswick: *www.gnb.ca/legis*
House of Assembly of Newfoundland and Labrador: *www.assembly.nl.ca*
Legislative Assembly of the Northwest Territories: *www.assembly.gov.nt.ca*
Legislative Assembly of Nova Scotia: *www.nslegislature.ca*
Legislative Assembly of Nunavut: *www.assembly.nu.ca*
Legislative Assembly of Ontario: *www.ontla.on.ca*
Legislative Assembly of Prince Edward Island: *www.assembly.pe.ca*
National Assembly of Quebec: *www.assnat.qc.ca*
Legislative Assembly of Saskatchewan: *www.legassembly.sk.ca*
Legislative Assembly of the Yukon: *www.legassembly.gov.yk.ca*

———————

OTHER IMPORTANT WEBSITES

Assembly of First Nations: *www.afn.ca*
The Canadian Forces: *www.forces.gc.ca*
The Canadian Royal Heritage Trust: *www.crht.ca*
Le Chemin du Roy: *www.lecheminduroy.com*
Dr. Christopher McCreery (Expert author on the Canadian Honours System):
    www.christophermccreery.com
La Citadelle (Official residence of the governor general located in Quebec City):
    www.lacitadelle.qc.ca

The Commonwealth Secretariat: *www.thecommonwealth.org*

Department of Canadian Heritage (section on Canadian Monarchy): *www.pch.gc.ca*

Duke of Edinburgh's Award: *www.dukeofed.org*

Her Majesty's Royal Chapel of the Mohawks: *www.mohawkchapel.ca*

The Hnatyshyn Foundation: *www.rjhf.com*

The Michaëlle Jean Foundation: *www.mjf-fmj.ca*

The Monarchist League of Canada: *www.monarchist.ca*

Their Royal Highnesses The Prince of Wales, The Duchess of Cornwall, Prince William and Prince Harry: *www.princeofwales.gov.uk*

The Prince's Trust: *www.princes-trust.org.uk*

The Prince of Wales Northern Heritage Centre: *www.pwnhc.ca*

Privy Council Office: *www.pco-bcp.gc.ca*

The Royal Heraldry Society: *www.heraldry.ca*

The Royal Society of Canada: *www.rsc.ca*

The Sauvé Scholars Program: *www.sauvescholars.org*

The United Empire Loyalists' Association of Canada: *www.uelac.org*

The Vanier Institute of the Family: *www.vifamily.ca*

DEFINITIONS

*These definitions have been reproduced with permission from *A Crown of Maples* by Kevin MacLeod (see citation in bibliography).

Armorial bearings
Distinguishing symbols or designs used by nations, governments, corporations, institutions, and individuals to indicate Sovereignty, authority, ownership, and identity. Also known as coats of arms.

British North America Act, 1867
A statute of the British Parliament in 1867 that provided for the creation of the Dominion of Canada. As Canada's original constitution (in 1982 renamed Constitution Act, 1867), it has been amended many times and, along with other legislative documents and decrees, forms an integral part of Canada's constitution.

Canadian Crown
All executive powers exercised by or on behalf of Her Majesty Queen Elizabeth II, as Queen of Canada, within our system of constitutional monarchy, which ensures effective and orderly government.

A member of the Royal 22e Régiment (the Van Doos) stands guard at La Citadelle, 2010. Photo by Roy and Greta Vanderwal.

Collective Crown

A term used to describe the institution comprised of the Sovereign (Queen Elizabeth II as Queen of Canada) and her eleven direct representatives: the governor general (federal jurisdiction) and the ten lieutenant governors (provincial jurisdictions).

Commonwealth

A free association of nations from around the world. All nations are equal partners, dedicated to co-operation in the interest of freedom and development, and recognize the Queen as Head of the Commonwealth.

Confederation

The union of the Province of Canada (Ontario and Quebec), Nova Scotia, and New Brunswick as provided for by the British North America Act, 1867 to form the Dominion of Canada.

Constitution Act, 1867

See British North America Act, 1867

Constitutional convention

Well-established customs or practices, which have evolved over time and are integral aspects of our system of government, even though they are not specifically mentioned in the constitution. One of three elements that make up Canada's constitution: written constitution, legislation, and unwritten constitution (rules of common law and conventions).

Constitutional monarchy

A form of government in which executive powers (Crown) are exercised by or on behalf of the Sovereign and on the basis of ministerial advice.

Court of Queen's Bench

The superior-court trial division in the provincial jurisdiction (New Brunswick, Manitoba, Saskatchewan, and Alberta). Different names are used in other provinces and territories. Nova Scotia, British Columbia, Prince Edward Island, Newfoundland, Northwest Territories, Yukon, and Nunavut all refer to it as the "Supreme Court"; Quebec employs "Superior Court"; and Ontario refers to it as "Ontario Court, General Division."

Crown of Canada

See Canadian Crown.

Crown corporations

Corporations in which the government, be it at the national or provincial level, has total or majority ownership. Organized on the pattern of private enterprises, they have a mandate to provide specific goods and/or services.

Crown land

Land belonging to the government, whether in the national or provincial jurisdiction.

Decorations for Bravery

Honours awarded to people who have incurred a grave risk of injury or have placed their lives in jeopardy in attempting to rescue others. These honours are awarded by the governor general on behalf of the Queen.

Dissolution of Parliament

The termination of the life of a Parliament, and by extension the ruling government, which is followed by a general election. Dissolution is proclaimed by the representative of the Queen on the advice of the prime minister or premier.

Equerry

An officer of the Canadian Forces appointed to attend the Queen or a member of the Royal family during a visit to Canada.

Executive

The branch of government that carries out the law — the Cabinet and ruling government that sit in the elected chamber (House of Commons/Legislature). Also referred to as "The Queen in Council."

Executive Council

The premier of the province and members of the Cabinet, which are akin to the Privy Council (prime minister and members of the Cabinet) in the federal jurisdiction.

Fathers of Confederation

The thirty-six delegates who, between 1864 and 1867, met to discuss terms of union for the British North American colonies that led in 1867 to the creation of the Dominion of Canada.

Federal state

A nation that brings together different political communities with a national government for common purposes and separate (provincial/state) governments for the particular purposes of each community.

Government House

Her Majesty's official residences in Canada, situated in Ottawa and most provincial capitals and occupied by the Queen's representative. Government House in Ottawa is known as Rideau Hall.

Governor

The personal representative of the French King who directed operations in New France on behalf of the French Crown. This function was in effect from 1627 until 1760. Subsequently, governors served as colonial administrators under the British Crown.

Governor General

The personal representative of the Queen who acts on her behalf in performing certain duties and responsibilities in the federal jurisdiction.

House of Commons

The elected, lower chamber of Canada's Parliament through which all legislation must pass before it becomes law. The members are chosen in general elections held every four years based on fixed election dates, pursuant to new legislation passed in 2007.

Judicial

The branch of government that interprets the law — in other words, the courts. Also referred to as "The Queen in Banco" or "The Queen on the Bench."

Legislative

The branch of government that makes the laws — Parliament of Canada/provincial and territorial legislatures. Also referred to as "The Queen in Parliament."

Legislature

The federal legislature (Parliament of Canada) consists of the Queen, the Senate, and the House of Commons. The provincial legislatures consist of the lieutenant governor and the elected house.

Letters of Credence

Formal letters accrediting Canadian ambassadors/particular high commissioners as the official representatives of Canada in foreign states.

Letters Patent:

A document issued by the Sovereign that serves as an instrument of conveyance or grant, in areas as diverse as land, franchises, and offices. The Letters Patent issued by King George VI in 1947 transferred most of the Sovereign's powers to the governor general to be exercised in Canada.

Lieutenant Governor

The personal representative of the Queen who acts on her behalf in performing certain duties and responsibilities in the provincial jurisdiction.

Mace
A staff, normally bearing a Crown, that rests in Canadian legislative chambers while the chambers are in session. The mace symbolizes the legitimate right of the legislatures to sit under authority of the Crown.

Magna Carta
The charter of English personal and political liberties granted by King John at Runnymede, England, in 1215.

Majority government
A government formed by the leader of the political party who has won a majority of seats in the House of Commons/legislature following a general election.

Meritorious Service Decorations (Military and Civil Decorations)
Honours awarded to Canadians or non-Canadians for a deed or activity performed in a professional manner or of a high standard that brings benefit or honour to the Canadian Forces or to Canada. These honours are awarded by the governor general on behalf of the Queen.

Ministers of the Crown
Members of a government who are selected by the prime minister/premier to be given cabinet responsibilities in specific areas and to be known as Cabinet ministers. The oath of office is administered in the presence of the Sovereign's representative.

Minority government
A government formed when no party holds a clear majority of seats in the House of Commons/legislature following a general election. Usually, the government is formed by the party with the most seats.

Order of Canada
Honours awarded to Canadians to recognize their achievement in important fields of

human endeavour and service to their country. These honours are awarded by the governor general on behalf of the Queen.

Order of Military Merit
Honours awarded to regular or reserve members of the Canadian Forces to recognize conspicuous merit and exceptional service. These honours are awarded by the governor general on behalf of the Queen.

Parliament of Canada
The supreme legislature of Canada consisting of the Queen (represented by the governor general), the Senate, and the House of Commons.

Parliamentary democracy
A British system of government in which the executive (prime minister/premier and Cabinet) sit in the elected chamber (House of Commons/Legislature) and are accountable to the elected representatives of the people. From time to time, members of the Executive (Ministers of the Crown) have sat in the upper chamber (the Senate).

Patriation of the Constitution
The 1982 process whereby the British Parliament divested itself of its power to amend the Canadian Constitution, and the Constitution Act, 1982, provided Canada with its own amending formula.

Premier
The first minister, or head, of a provincial government, who is also the leader of the party in power.

Prerogative powers
Those powers of the Crown that are based in constitutional convention — discretionary authority exercised by the Crown. See also Royal prerogative.

Prime Minister
The first minister, or head, of a federal government, who is also the leader of the party in power.

Privy Council
The prime minister and members of the Cabinet — the equivalent of the Executive Council (premier and members of the Cabinet) in the provincial jurisdiction.

Republic
A nation with an elected or nominated president who may serve as both head of government and head of state, or simply as head of state.

Reserve powers
Powers that remain vested in the Crown that can be used by the Queen and her representatives (governor general and lieutenant governors) in special situations.

Responsible government
A government that is responsible to the people, based on the principle that governments must be responsible to the representatives of the people.

Royal Assent
The consent granted by the Queen's representative (governor general or lieutenant governor), which serves as the Crown's approval of a bill, thereby making it an act (law).

Royal Prerogative
The historic rights and privileges from which flow all executive powers (the Crown) as exercised by the Sovereign.

Royal commissions
Official inquiries into matters of public concern that have their historic origin within the Sovereign's prerogative powers to order investigations.

Senate

The appointed upper chamber of Canada's Parliament through which all legislation must pass before it becomes law.

Sovereign

One who reigns over a state or territory, usually by hereditary right, and often (such as in Canada) within the limits — or rules — of a constitution. a.k.a. the king, queen, or monarch.

Speech from the Throne

A statement of work being proposed by the government to be undertaken in the parliamentary session being opened. The speech is prepared by the government and read by the governor general or the lieutenant governor. In Quebec, the Speech from the Throne is read by the premier in the presence of the lieutenant governor.

Statute of Westminster, 1931

A law of the British Parliament (December 11, 1931) that granted Canada and other dominions full legal independence and legislative autonomy, thus ending Britain's overriding authority over Dominion legislation.

Statutory powers

Powers that are written in law.

Victoria Day

A national holiday established by Parliament in 1901 and observed on the first Monday preceding May 25. Originally intended to honour the birthday of Queen Victoria, the day now celebrates the birthday of Queen Elizabeth II (although the actual date is April 21).

Vote of non-confidence

A vote on a motion that indicates that the government has lost the confidence of the House if it is adopted. The government would then normally resign or request the governor general/lieutenant governor to dissolve Parliament/Legislature and issue election writs.

BIBLIOGRAPHY

Arbuckle, J. Graeme. *Badges of the Canadian Navy*. Halifax: Nimbus Publishing Limited, 1987.

Arbuckle, Lieutenant (N) Graeme. *Customs and Traditions of the Canadian Navy*. Halifax: Nimbus Publishing Limited, 1984.

Archbold, Rick. *I Stand For Canada: The Story of the Maple Leaf Flag*. Toronto: MacFarlane Walter & Ross, 2002.

Arnot, David. (10 June 2010). *The Honour of First Nations — The Honour of the Crown: The Unique Relationship of First Nations with the Crown*. Unpublished paper presented at The Crown in Canada: Present Realities and Future Options, Ottawa. *www.queensu.ca/iigr/conf/ConferenceOnTheCrown.html*.

Bagehot, Walter. *The English Constitution*. 1867. Reprint, London: Oxford University Press, 1991.

Bousfield, Arthur and Garry Toffoli. *Royal Spring: The Royal Tour of 1939 and The Queen Mother in Canada*. Toronto: Dundurn Press, 1989.

Bousfield, Arthur and Garry Toffoli. *Home to Canada: Royal Tours 1786–2010*. Toronto: Dundurn Press, 2010.

Boyce, Peter. *The Queen's Other Realms: The Crown and Its Legacy in Australia, Canada and New Zealand*. Sydney: The Federation Press, 2009.

Bradford, Sarah. *Elizabeth: A Biography of Her Majesty the Queen*. Toronto: Key Porter Books, 1996.

Brooks, Stephen. *Canadian Democracy: An Introduction*. Toronto: Oxford University Press, 1996.

Buckie, Catherine. *Parliamentary Democracy in Nova Scotia: How it Began, How it Evolved*. Halifax: Office of the Speaker, 2008.

Buckner, Phillip ed. *Canada and the End of Empire*. Vancouver: University of British Columbia Press, 2005.

Canada. Department of Indian and Northern Affairs. *Why do Governments Negotiate Treaties with Aboriginal Peoples?* Ottawa: Minister of Indian Affairs and Northern Development, 2004.

Canada. Department of National Defence. *Queen's Regulations and Orders for the Canadian Forces*. 6.04, Ottawa: Queen's Printer for Canada, 2008.

Canada. Royal Commission on Aboriginal Peoples. Report. 5 Vols. Ottawa: Minister of Supply and Services Canada, 1996.

Canada's Parliament. Ottawa: House of Commons, 1973.

Carney, Pat. *Tiara & Atigi: Northwest Territories 1970 Centennial*. Vancouver: Mitchell Press Limited, 1971.

Cheffins, Ronald I. "The Royal Prerogative and the Office of Lieutenant Governor." *Canadian Parliamentary Review* (Spring 2000): 1419.

Edward, Duke of Windsor. *A King's Story: The Memories of the Duke of Windsor*. New York: Thomas Allen, 1951.

Fischer, David Hackett. *Champlain's Dream*. Toronto: Alfred A. Knopf Canada, 2008.

Forsey, Eugene A. *How Canadians Govern Themselves: Sixth Edition*. Ottawa: Government of Canada, 2005.

Fowler Jr., William M. *Empires at War*. Vancouver: Douglas & McIntyre, 2005.

Francis, R. Douglas, Richard Jones, and Donald B. Smith. *Origins: Canadian History to Confederation, Sixth Edition*. Toronto: Nelson Education, 2009.

Francis, Mayann E. Remarks by Her Honour The Honourable Mayann E. Francis, Lieutenant Governor of Nova Scotia. Treaty Day Ceremony. Halifax, October 1, 2007.

Fraser, John. "Do we Still Care?" *Maclean's* (November 29, 2010): 88–87.

Fraser, John. *Eminent Canadians: Candid Tales of Then and Now.* Toronto: McClelland & Stewart, 2000.

Fraser, John. "Who will be King of Canada?" *Maclean's* (April 29, 2011).

Fryer, Mary Beacock and Christopher Dracott. *John Graves Simcoe, 1752–1806: A Biography.* Toronto: Dundurn Press, 1998.

Funston, Bernard and Eugene Meehan. *Canadian Constitutional Documents Consolidated.* Toronto: Carswell, 1994.

Grant, Shelagh D. *Polar Imperative: The History of Arctic Sovereignty in North America.* Toronto: Douglas & McIntyre, 2010.

Greaves, Kevin. *A Canadian Heraldic Primer.* Ottawa: Heraldry Society of Canada, 2000.

Hennessey, Catherine G., David Keenlyside, and Edward MacDonald. *The Landscapes of Confederation: Charlottetown, 1864.* Charlottetown: Museum & Heritage, 2010.

Hnatyshyn, Gerda. *Rideau Hall: Canada's Living Heritage.* Vanier: Friends of Rideau Hall, 1994.

Howarth, Patrick. *George VI.* London: Hutchinson, 1987.

Inside Canada's Parliament: An Introduction to how the Canadian Parliament Works. Ottawa: Library of Parliament, 2002.

Jackson, D. Michael. *The Canadian Monarchy in Saskatchewan.* Regina: Government of Saskatchewan, 1990.

Jackson, D. Michael. *Royal Saskatchewan: The Crown in a Canadian Province.* Regina: Government of Saskatchewan, 2007.

Jackson, D. Michael and Lynda Haverstock. (10 June 2010). *The Crown in the Provinces: Canada's Compound Monarchy.* Unpublished paper presented at The Crown in Canada: Present Realities and Future Options, Ottawa. *www.queensu.ca/iigr/conf/ConferenceOnTheCrown.html.*

Jerome, James. *Mr. Speaker.* Toronto: McClelland & Stewart Limited, 1985.

Joyal, Serge. (9 June 2010). *The Crown and Prime Ministerial Government.* Unpublished paper presented at The Crown in Canada: Present Realities and Future Options, Ottawa. *www.queensu.ca/iigr/conf/ConferenceOnTheCrown.html.*

Langdon, H.H. and George M. Wrong, eds. *The Chronicles of Canada: Volume VIII — The Growth of Nationality.* Arizona: Fireship Press, 2009.

Lennox, Doug. *Now You Know Royalty.* Toronto: Dundurn Press, 2009.

MacKinnon, Frank. *The Crown in Canada*. Calgary: McClelland & Stewart West, 1976.

MacLeod, Kevin. *A Crown of Maples: Constitutional Monarchy in Canada*. Ottawa: Department of Canadian Heritage, 2008.

Macnutt, James W. *Building for Democracy*. Halifax: Formac Publishing Company Limited, 2010.

Matheson, John Ross. *Canada's Flag: A Search for a Country*. Boston: G.K. Hall and Company, 1980.

McCreery, Christopher. *On Her Majesty's Service*. Toronto: Dundurn Press, 2008.

McCreery, Christopher. *The Beginner's Guide to Honours*. Toronto: Dundurn Press, 2008.

McCreery, Christopher. *The Canadian Forces' Decoration*. Ottawa: Department of National Defence, 2009.

McCreery, Christopher. *The Canadian Honours System*. Toronto: Dundurn Press, 2005.

McCreery, Christopher. *The Order of Canada: Its Origins, History, and Development*. Toronto: Dundurn Press, 2006.

McWhinney, Edward. *The Governor General and the Prime Ministers*. Vancouver: Ronsdale Press, 2005.

Monahan, Patrick J. *Constitutional Law: Third Edition*. Toronto: Irwin Law, 2006.

Monet, Jacques. *The Canadian Crown*. Toronto: Clarke & Company Limited, 1979.

Monet, Jacques, ed. *Jules Léger: A Selection of his Writings on Canada*. Ottawa: La Presse, 1982.

The Ontario Gazette. Vol. 137, No. 27 (July 3, 2004).

Pachter, Charles. *M is For Moose: A Charles Pachter Alphabet*. Toronto: Cormorant Books, 2008.

"Prince Charles Honored with HMS's Global Citizen Award." *Harvard Gazette*, February 1, 2007.

Radforth, Ian Walter. *Royal Spectacle: The 1860 Visit of the Prince of Wales to Canada*. Toronto: University of Toronto Press, 2004.

Reid, Marion L. *These Roots Run Deep*. Charlottetown: Tangle Lane, 2005.

Reynolds, Ken. *Pro Valore: Canada's Victoria Cross, Revised Edition*. Ottawa: Government of Canada, 2009.

Russell, Peter and Lorne Sossin, eds. *Parliamentary Democracy in Crisis*. Toronto: University of Toronto Press, 2009.

Saskatchewan Royal Reflections: The Prince of Wales in Saskatchewan April 2001. Regina: Department of Intergovernmental and Aboriginal Affairs, 2001.

Senate of Canada. *Canada A Constitutional Monarchy*. Ottawa: Senate of Canada, 2004.

Smith, David E. *The Invisible Crown: The First Principle of Canadian Government*. Toronto: University of Toronto Press, 1995.

Smith, David E. *The People's House of Commons*. Toronto: University of Toronto Press, 2007.

Stamp, Robert M. *Kings, Queens and Canadians*. Markham: Fitzhenry & Whiteside Limited, 1987.

Swan, Conrad. *Canada: Symbols of Sovereignty*. Toronto: University of Toronto Press, 1977.

Symons, Thomas H.B. *To Know Ourselves: The Report of the Commission on Canadian Studies*. Ottawa: Association of Universities and Colleges of Canada, 1975.

Taylor, Charles. *Sources of the Self: The Making of the Modern Identity*. Cambridge: Harvard University Press, 1992.

The Constitution Acts: 1867 to 1982. Ottawa: Department of Justice, 2001.

The Liquidators of the Maritime Bank of Canada vs. The Receiver General of New Brunswick, (1892) A.C. 437.

Vance, Jonathan F. *A History of Canadian Culture*. Toronto: Oxford University Press, 2009.

Weston, Hilary. *No Ordinary Time*. Toronto: Whitfield Editions, 2007.

Wheeler-Bennett, John W. *King George VI: His Life and Reign*. Toronto: MacMillan, 1958.

INDEX

Aarand, Argo, 154

Acadians, Acadia 23, 28–30, 33

Agricultural Merit Award, *see* Province of
Quebec

Aide-de-camp, as role, 21, 218, 240

Albert, Prince (consort to Queen Victoria), 210

Alberta, Province of, 19, 28, 44, 76, 95, 98,
103, 105, 106, 115–18, 144, 146–48, 163,
168, 171, 181–83, 191–93, 208, 217, 218,
220, 224, 227, 228, 232, 240, 258
Alberta Order of Excellence, 163

Alexander, The Honourable Lincoln, 120, 207

Alexander, Sir William, 213–14

Alexandra, Princess (daughter of the late
Duke and the Duchess of Kent), as
colonel-in-chief, 151

Alfred, Prince (son of Queen Victoria), 216

American Revolution, American
Revolutionary War, 32, 117, 134, 135,
138, 141, 209, 224

Amherst, Lord Jeffery (1st Baron Amherst),
31, 118, 238

Amherstburg, Ontario, 18

Ancient and Honourable Hyack Anvil Battery
Salute, 209–10

Andrew, Prince (Duke of York), 110, 113,
148, 155, 181, 184, 216, 226
As colonel-in-chief, 148

Anishinabe/Anishinabeg, 125, 134–35

Annapolis Royal (Port Royal), Nova Scotia,
27, 29, 115, 197

Anne, Princess (Princess Royal), 181, 184
As colonel-in-chief, 147–48

Anne, Queen, 115, 131, 132, 138
Queen Anne Chapel, Mohawk Valley,
138, 140

Antigua and Barbuda, West Indies, 201, 206

Arctic Archipelago, 44

Armorial Bearings (Coat of Arms), 32, 82, 172, 175, 225
Arnold, Benedict, 218
Arnot, Justice David, 127
Arthur, Prince (Duke of Connaught), 115, 216, 228
Athlone, 1st Earl, (Major-General Alexander Cambridge), 117, 118, 217, 238
Aurora, Ontario, 197
Australia, Commonwealth of, 46, 47, 201, 204, 206, 228

Baden-Powell, Lieutenant General Robert Stephenson Smyth, 91
Bagehot, Walter, 84, 97, 206
Baldwin, Robert, 37, 38
Balfour Report (1926), 46
Ballantyne, Corporal Jim, 60
Balmoral Castle (Scotland), 128
Barbados, West Indies, 202, 204, 206
Baron de Longueuil (Charles le Moyne de Longueuil), 211
    List of Barons de Longueuil, 211–12
Battle of Moraviantown (1813), *see* War of 1812–14
Battle of Passchendaele, *see* First World War
Battle of Vimy Ridge, *see* First World War
Bay of Quinte, Ontario, 135, 140
Beatty, Bruce, 154
Bennett, The Right Honourable Richard B., 224
    1st Viscount Bennett, 212
Black Rod in the Senate, 71, 77, 78, 240-43
    Usher of Black Rod, 71, 78, 241–43
    List of Ushers of the Black Rod in the Senate, 242

Blood Tribe (Alberta), 217, 218
Boudreau, Claire, (Chief Herald of Canada), 170, 176, 177, 245
Bousfield, Arthur, 34
Brant, Captain Joseph, 134–35
Brantford, Ontario, 138, 140, 182
British Colonial Office, 44
British Columbia, Colony of, 28, 39
British Columbia, Province of, 17, 19, 39, 76, 96–98, 101, 103, 115, 116, 118, 119, 122, 123, 127, 141, 147, 151, 163, 165, 181, 182, 208, 210, 218–20, 225, 245, 246, 258
    Order of British Columbia, 165
British Commonwealth Air Training Program, 232
British Crown, 28, 31–34, 36, 47, 58, 126, 140, 212, 259 (*see also* Canadian Crown)
British Empire, 38, 42, 46, 47, 79, 200, 201, 228
British North America, 28, 36, 37, 40, 42, 134, 135, 259
British North America Act (1867), 42, 58, 255
    see also Constitution Act (1867)
British Parliament, 46, 47, 51, 255, 257, 262, 264
    Statute of Westminster (1931), 46–48, 55, 57, 200, 264

Caboto, Giovanni (John Cabot), 23, 76
Cadieux, Dolphus, 61
Callbeck, The Honourable Phillips, 218–19
Campbell, Gordon (Premier), 17
Camilla, Duchess of Cornwall, 224–25
    Patron of Dundurn Castle National Historic Site, 225
Canada, Province of 38, 192, 257
    Canada East, 39, 40, 41

Canada West, 39, 40, 224
Canadian Border Services Agency, 170
Canadian Brigades Group, 185
Canadian Canoe Museum (Peterborough), 110, 113
Canadian Coat of Arms, 222
Canadian Broadcasting Corporation, 222
Canadian Business for Social Responsibility (CBSR), 197
Canadian Constitution, 54–69, 125, 128, 262
Canadian Cancer Society, 120
Canadian Citizenship Act (1947), 49
Canadian Coast Guard:
    CCGS *Sir William Alexander*, 214
Canadian Crown, 19, 20, 38, 79–80, 92, 101, 113, 118, 128, 133, 175, 211, 212, 255
Canadian Equerry to the Queen, as a role, 243–45, 258
Canadian Football League, 121, 224
    Grey Cup, 121
Canadian Forces, 82, 84, 85, 141–43, 152, 261–62
    Canadian Forces Base (CFB), 195, 208
    Canadian Forces' Decoration, 155
    Canadian Rangers, 151
Canadian Heraldic Authority, 62, 169–178, 211, 245
    Badges of Office, 176–78
    Chief Herald of Canada, 170, 174, 176, 245
    Deputy Herald Chancellor, 174
    Herald, 169, 170, 172–78, 245
    Heraldry, 25, 169, 172, 174, 177
Canadian Honours System, 153–56
    Commemorative Medals, 155
    Decorations, 155
    Long Service Medals, 155
    Medals, 155–56
    Most Venerable Order of the Hospital of St. John of Jerusalem, 162
    Order of Canada, 157–58
    Order of Merit, 161
    Order of Merit of the Police Forces, 159
    Order of Military Merit, 158
    Provincial Honours, 162
    Provincial Orders, 163–68
Canadian Grenadier Guards, 85–86, 146
Canadian Interuniversity Sport Football (Vanier Cup), 122
Canadian Museum for Human Rights (Winnipeg) 76, 130, 183
Canadian International Dragon Boat Festival (Ramon John Hnatyshyn Cup), 123
Canadian Rangers, *see* Canadian Forces
Canadian Secretary to the Queen, 71, 179, 234 (*see also* Kevin MacLeod)
Canadian Senior Golf Association (Devonshire Cup), 122
Canadian Sovereigns, 230, 233–37
    British Crown, 235
    Canadian Crown, 235, 237
    English Crown, 233, 235
    French Crown, 233
Canadian State Visit, 187
Canadian Youth Business Foundation, 197
Canadian Victoria Cross, 76, 155, 208
Canadian Warplane Heritage Museum (Hamilton, Ontario), 152
Cartier, Sir George-Étienne, 40, 41, 218, 226
Cartier, Jacques, 23–25, 225
Catherine, Duchess of Cambridge, 2, 19, 124, 128, 151, 183, 184, 198, 199, 232

Cavagnial, Pierre de Rigaud de Vaudreuil de
    (Marquis de Vaudreuil), 31, 82, 238
Cayuga, *see* Iroquois Confederacy
Champlain, Samuel de, 26, 27, 82, 118, 125,
    126, 226, 237
Chapel Royal, 137, 138, 140
Charles I, King of Great Britain, 39, 115, 117,
    118, 213, 235
Charles II, King of Great Britain, 28, 235
Charles, Prince of Wales, 17, 19, 70, 104, 110,
    112, 116, 122, 124, 127, 141, 147, 149,
    152, 155, 181, 184, 189, 190, 195–97, 199,
    218, 224, 225, 226, 249
    As colonel-in-chief, 147
    As patron, 112, 152, 197
    Charities, 197
    Personal Canadian Flag, 195
    Prince of Wales Prize for Municipal
        Heritage Leadership, 196
Charlotte, Queen (consort to George III),
    115, 116, 216
Charlottetown, 116, 148, 152, 180, 181
    Flag, 116
Charlottetown Conference (1864), 20, 36,
    39–41, 180
Charter of Rights and Freedoms (1982), *see*
    Constitutional Act of 1982
Chaste, Aymar de, 26, 237
Château Frontenac (Quebec City), 117
Chatelaine, as title, 245
Chemin du Roy (The King's Road, Quebec), 223–24
Chief Herald of Canada, *see* Canadian
    Heraldic Authority
Chrétien, The Right Honourable Jean, 160–61
Chrétien, Aline, 160

Christmas tree, tradition of, 210
Churchill, The Right Honourable, Sir Winston, 218
Clarke, Garry, 246
Clarke, The Honourable Glen, 98
Clarkson, The Right Honourable Adrienne,
    88, 120, 123, 217, 239
    Clarkson Cup, *see* National Canadian
        Women's Hockey Championship
    Governor General's Northern Medal, 88
    Institute for Canadian Citizenship, 120
Coat of Arms, *see* Armorial Bearings
Commission on Canadian Studies (1976), 18–19
Commander-in-Chief, as role, 84–85, 143
    Commander-in-Chief Unit
        Commendation, 85
Commonwealth of Nations, 47, 50, 61, 151,
    152, 161, 200, 201, 204, 209, 210, 212,
    215, 218, 241, 257
    Commonwealth Games, 76, 181, 182, 207
    Commonwealth heads of government, 181
    Commonwealth Secretariat, 200
    Members of the Commonwealth, 210–03
Commonwealth Realm, 205, 206
Confederation, 16, 17, 20, 23, 24, 36, 39–42,
    45, 71, 76, 81, 94, 95, 98, 99, 103, 155,
    163, 180–82, 190, 193, 214, 230, 257
    Centennial of, 1967, 180, 228
    Confederation Medal (1867), 208
    Fathers of Confederation, 20, 23, 36, 95, 259
Constitution:
    Written, 56, 58, 69, 248, 257
    Unwritten, 57, 58, 66, 68, 69, 95, 248, 257
Constitution Act of 1791, 37
Constitution Act (1867), 42, 58, 62, 64, 84, 94,
    162, 255, 257

Constitution Act of 1982, 50, 51, 76, 97, 182, 262
    Charter of Rights and Freedoms, 51, 57
Covenants (treaties), 126–31, 135, 136
Crosby, The Honourable John C., 95
Crown Corporation, 258
Crown jewels, 220
Crown land, 258
Crown Royal Whisky, 217
Currie, General Sir Arthur (Canadian Corps), 218

Decorations, *see* Canadian Honours System
Department of Canadian Heritage, *see* Executive
Deputy Herald Chancellor, *see* Canadian Heraldic Authority
Deseronto, Chief John (Mohawk), 135
Deseronto, Ontario, 138
Devonshire Cup, *see* Canadian Senior Golf Association
Dexter, Premier Darrell, 64
Diana, Princess of Wales, 110, 191
Dorchester, Lord (Sir Guy Carleton, 1st Baron Dorchester), 238
Douglas, The Honourable James, 39, 134, 217
Dufferin, The Earl of (Frederick Hamilton-Temple-Blackwood, 1st Marquess of Dufferin), 25, 44, 86, 89, 92, 118, 239
Dundas, Ontario, 218
Dundas, The Honourable Henry, 218
Duchess of Gloucester (Birgitte Eva van Deurs Henriksen), as colonel-in-chief, 148
Duke of Cambridge, *see* Prince William
Duke of Edinburgh, *see* Prince Philip
Duke of Edinburgh's Awards, *see* Prince Philip

Duke of Kent (Prince Richard), as colonel-in-chief, 148
Duke of Kent (1767–1820), *see* Prince Edward
Duke of York, *see* Prince Andrew
Dundurn Castle National Historic Site (Hamilton), 225

Edward, Prince (Duke of Kent, 1767–1820), 34–36, 220, 226
    As commander-in-chief, 36, 148, 220
Edward, Prince (Earl of Wessex), 115, 181, 184
    As colonel-in-chief, 148
Edward I, King, 55, 237
Edward VII, King, 108, 116, 138, 161, 228, 236
    As Prince of Wales, 90, 190, 192, 208, 216, 219, 228
Edward VIII, King of Great Britain and Ireland, 143, 145, 193, 226, 228–31, 236
    As Prince Edward (Prince of Wales), 180, 192–93, 218, 224, 228, 230
    As Duke of Windsor, 227–28
Elizabeth, Queen (consort to King George VI, later Queen Mother), 49, 107, 143, 147, 151, 217, 219, 220, 226, 230
Elizabeth I, Queen of England, 25, 115, 116, 118, 235
Elizabeth II, Queen of Canada, 7, 16, 20, 49–52, 59, 63, 70–80, 106–08, 111, 117, 126, 128, 132, 140, 142, 143, 146, 170, 174, 193, 194, 198, 200, 201, 204–06, 208, 211, 216, 218, 221, 222, 224, 226, 228, 237, 243, 256, 257, 264
    As air commodore-in-chief, 151
    As captain-general, 151
    As colonel-in-chief, 144, 146

As commander-in-chief, 143
As colonel-in-chief, 144, 146
As patron to, 151
As Princess Elizabeth, 110, 193, 194, 219, 220
Head of the Commonwealth, 50, 200–04, 257
Queen Elizabeth II Jubilee Medals, 155–56
Elliot, Griffin, 21
EP Ranch (Pekisko, Alberta), 192, 193, 227–28
Ethell, The Honourable Donald Stewart, 98
Executive Council, 37, 37, 38, 58
Department of Canadian Heritage, 108

Fedoruk, The Honourable Dr. Sylvia, 211
First Nations University (Saskatchewan), 128–29
First Poppy, see Remembrance Day
First World War, 225, 230
Battle of Passchendaele, 225
Battle of Vimy Ridge, 76, 146, 218
Fischer, David Hackett, 26
Forks National Historic Site, The (Winnipeg), 136
Forsey, Senator Eugene, 23
Fountain of Hope, see Rideau Hall
Fox, Terry, 224
Francis, The Honourable Mayann E., 64, 96, 101
François I, King of France, 23, 24, 225, 233
Fraser, John (Massey College), 19, 179
French and Indian Wars (aka The Seven Years'
War/La guerre de la Conquête), 30–31
French Crown, 28, 29, 31, 82, 125, 126, 128,
131, 133, 233, 259
Frobisher, Martin, 25

George II, King of Great Britain, 29, 117, 137,
209, 216, 235
George III, King of Great Britain, 31, 32, 108,
115, 116, 132, 133, 135, 216, 226, 235
Royal Proclamation (1763), 32, 132–34
George IV, King of Great Britain, 116, 135, 235
George V, King of Great Britain, 46, 48, 90, 91, 108,
109, 116, 117, 218, 219, 222, 224, 235, 250
As Duke of Cornwall and York, 192, 219
George VI, King of Great Britain and Canada,
49, 66, 82, 108, 111, 143, 151, 155, 192,
203, 217, 219, 220, 226, 230, 236, 237, 260
As Duke of York, 222
As Prince Albert, 192
Royal tour 1939, 49, 230
George, Prince (Duke of Kent, 1902–1942), 193
Gilbert, Humphrey, 25
Golf Canada, 208, see also Royal Canadian
Association
Golf Canada Championship (Willingdon
Cup), 122
Gourlay, Travis, 21
Governor General's Awards and Medals, 86–89
Academic Medal (Lord Dufferin), 86
Awards for Excellence in Teaching
Canadian History (National History
Society), 87
Award in Celebration of the Nation's
Table (Michaëlle Jean), 88–89
Awards in Commemoration of the
Person's Case, 87
Awards in Visual and Media Arts
(Roméo LeBlanc), 88
Caring Canadian Award (Roméo
LeBlanc), 87
International Award for Canadian
Studies, 87–88
Literary Awards (Lord Tweedsmuir), 86

Medals in Architecture (Massey Medals), 87

Michener Award (Roland Michener), 87

Northern Medal (Adrienne Clarkson), 88

Performing Arts Awards (Ramon J. Hnatyshyn), 86

Grant, Dr. Michael (12th Baron de Longueuil), 211–12

Great Seal of Canada

Queen Elizabeth II, 54

Queen Victoria, 42

Great Silver Seal (Prince Edward Island), 218

Grey Cup, *see* Canadian Football League

Grey, The Right Honourable Albert Henry George (4th Earl Grey), 91, 118, 239

Hagerman, The Honourable Barbara A., 100

Hamilton-Temple-Blackwood, The Right Honourable Frederick (1st Marquess of Dufferin), *see* the Earl of Dufferin

Harris, Chief Justice Robert E., 208

Harry, Prince, 104, 122, 151, 208

Hatley Castle (British Columbia), 219–20

Haudenosaunee Mohawk First Nation, *see* Iroquois Confederacy

Haverstock, The Honourable Dr. Lynda, 94

Head of the Commonwealth, 203–04, *see also* Queen Elizabeth II

Henri IV, King of France, 25–27, 226, 233

Henry VII, King of England, 23, 233

Her Majesty's Chapel Royal of the Mohawk (Christ Church) (Deseronto, Ontario), 138

Her Majesty's Royal Chapel of the Mohawks (St. Paul's) (Brantford, Ontario), 138

High Commission, 204

High Commissioners, 82, 204, 260

HMCS *Calgary*, 98

HMCS Royal Roads, *see* Hatley Castle

HMCS *St. John's*, 7

Hnatyshyn, The Right Honourable Ramon John, 85, 86, 88, 120, 123, 239

Hnatyshyn Foundation, 120

Ramon Hnatyshyn Cup, 123

House of Commons, *see also* Parliament of Canada

Majority government, 45, 261

Minority government, 45, 261

Howe, The Honourable Sir Joseph, 38

Howland, The Honourable Sir William P., 214

Hudson, Henry, 28

Hudson's Bay Company, 28, 39, 43, 44, 134

Hundred Associates (Company of New France), 27

Indian Act (1876), 135–36

Iroquois Confederacy (Haudenosaunee), 131,135

Cayuga, 33, 135

Mohawk, 33, 131, 132, 135, 138, 140

Onondaga, 33, 135

Jackson, Dr. Michael D., 21, 79, 94

James II, King of Great Britain, 117

James VI, King of Scotland (James I of Great Britain), 213, 235

Jean, The Right Honourable Michaëlle, 53, 83, 85, 88, 113, 120, 123, 124, 187, 239, 245

Michaëlle Jean Foundation, 120, 254

Jeanne Sauvé Cup, *see* National Ringette League

Jeffreys, C.W., 48

Jerome, The Honourable James, 63

John I, King of England, 54, 261

Magna Carta (1215), 54, 55, 130, 261

John, Prince (son of George V), 116

Johnston, The Right Honourable David, 81, 84, 85, 90, 120, 152, 184, 239
Johnson, Gordon, 215
Joyal, Senator Serge, 7, 83, 267
Judicial Committee of the British Privy Council, 45, 87, 94
Junior Men's champion lacrosse team (Canadian Lacrosse Association) (Minto Cup), 121

Kainai Chieftainship of the Blood Tribe, *see* Lord Tweedsmuir
Karsh, Yousuf, 139
King-Byng Crisis (1926), 45–46
King George's War (1744–1748), 29
King, The Right Honourable William Lyon Mackenzie, 66, 161, 217, 230
Kowalsky, The Honourable Myron (Speaker), 70

La Citadelle (Quebec City), 92, 217, 253, 256
Lady Byng Memorial Trophy, *see* National Hockey League
Lafontaine, Sir Louis-Hippolyte, 37–38
Lakefield College School (Lakefield, Ontario) 226
Lam, The Honourable David, 97, 123
Lambton, John (1st Earl of Durham), 37, 238
Lord Durham's Report (1818), 37
Lavallée, Calixa, 89
Laval, Monsigneur François de, 208
Lawrence, Major Charles, 30
Léger, The Right Honourable Jules, 83, 239
Leopold, Prince (son of Queen Victoria), 216
Letters Patent Constituting the Office of the Governor General (1947), 49–50, 82, 260
Liquidators of the Maritime Bank of Canada vs. The Receiver General of New

Brunswick, 45
London Conference (1866–67), 42
London Declaration (1949), 200, 203
Long Service Medals, *see* Canadian Honours System
Longueuil, Charles le Moyne de, 211
Lord Durham, *see* John Lambton
Lorjé, Pat, 189
Lorne, Marquess of Lorne (John Douglas Campbell), 89, 115, 118, 120, 192, 216, 220, 224, 239
Royal Society of Canada, 120
Louis XIII, King of France, 27, 82, 233
Louis XIV, King of France, 27, 82, 208, 211, 226, 233
Louis XV, King of France, 27, 31, 115, 223, 224, 233
Louisbourg, Fortress of, 25, 28, 29, 182
Louise, Princess (Marchioness of Lorne and Duchess of Argyll), 115, 116, 144, 147, 192, 216, 220, 224, 226
Lower Canada, Province of, 34, 36, 37, 214, 226
Loyalist, *see* United Empire Loyalist

Majority Government, *see* House of Commons
Malliki, Paul, 61
Manitoba, Province of, 19, 28, 44, 55, 76, 101, 115, 116, 130, 147, 166, 181–83, 220, 228, 245, 246, 258
Order of Manitoba, 166
McCrae, Lieutenant-Colonel John, 152
McGregor, Helen (Principal), 21
McGregor, The Honourable James Duncan, 220
McGuinty, The Honourable Dalton, 185

McKinnon, Professor Frank, 21, 65
McLaren, Mary C., 242
Memberton, Grand Chief Henri, 126
Meighen, The Right Honourable Arthur, 46
Michener, The Right Honourable Roland, 7, 60, 85, 87, 91, 157, 161, 239
Michener Award, 87
Middleton, Catherine, *see* Duchess of Cambridge
Middleton, Peter, 232
Mi'kmaq First Nation, 125, 126, 137
Mi'kmaw Treaty Day, 137
Milliken, The Honourable Peter, 221, 247
Miller, The Honourable Dan, 98
Miller, Robert J., 228
Minority Government, *see* House of Commons
Minto Cup, *see* The Earl of Minto
Mohawk First Nation, *see* Iroquois Confederacy
Mohawk Valley, 132, 138, 140
Monck, Lord, (Charles Stanley, 4th Viscount Monck), 92, 239
Monet, Jacques (s.j.), 13, 21, 77, 157
Montcalm, Louis-Joseph (Marquis de Saint-Veran), 31
Montreal, Quebec, 31, 33, 34, 76, 118, 146, 147, 180, 181, 192, 217, 224, 234
Moore, Sister Dorothy, 126
Most Noble Order of the Garter, *see* Vincent Massey
Most Venerable Order of the Hospital of St. John of Jerusalem, *see* Canadian Honours System
Musqua, Elder Danny (Saulteaux), 127

Nasogaluak, Bill, 61
National Assembly (Quebec), *see* Provincial Parliaments

National Canadian Women's Hockey Championship (Clarkson Cup), 123
National Gallery (Ottawa), 89
National Hockey League:
    Lady Byng Memorial Trophy), 122
    Prince of Wales Trophy, 228
    Stanley Cup, 121
National Ringette League (Jeanne Sauvé Cup), 122
National War Memorial (Ottawa), 143, 151
New Brunswick, Province of, 30, 33, 36, 39, 42, 45, 78, 95, 101, 103, 115, 116, 118, 146, 147, 182, 183, 192, 195, 211, 214, 246, 251, 257, 258
    Order of New Brunswick, 167
New France, 25–28, 31, 92, 132, 162, 208, 211, 223, 225, 237, 259
New York City, 201, 209
New York, State of, 107, 109, 117, 138
Newfoundland, Colony of, 34, 40, 41, 115, 213, 214,192
Newfoundland, Dominion of, 46–47
Newfoundland, Island of, 23, 25, 31, 76
Newfoundland and Labrador, Province of, 19, 64, 95, 103, 116, 114, 118, 148, 181, 182, 218, 258
    Order of Newfoundland and Labrador, 168
Newfoundland Constabulary, 106 (*see also* Royal Newfoundland Constabulary [RNC])
Niagara Peninsula, Ontario, 192
Northwest Passage, 25, 44
Northwest Territories, 28, 44, 61, 76, 110, 116, 117, 181, 195, 220, 258
North West Mounted Police, 107
Nova Scotia, Colony of, 20, 29, 30, 34, 36, 38, 39, 192, 213, 214, 216, 226

Nova Scotia, Province of, 19, 28, 29, 33, 35, 42, 60,
    64, 75, 96, 101, 102, 115, 116, 118, 137, 182,
    183, 208–10, 213, 216, 245, 246, 257, 258
    Flag (banner of arms), 39
    Order of Nova Scotia, 167
Nunavut, 28, 61, 116, 117, 123 , 131, 174, 182,
    226, 258
    The Nunavut Act (1993), 69
Nunqingaq, Mathew, 61

"O Canada" (anthem), 89
Oath of Citizenship, 70
Obama, President Barack, 83
Ohio Valley, 31
Onley, The Honourable David C., 21, 185, 186
Onley, Mrs. Ruth Ann, 186
Onondaga, see Iroquois Confederacy
Ontario, Province of, 19, 21, 33, 42, 60, 65,
    68, 102, 107, 109, 110, 115, 116, 118, 120,
    134, 138, 144, 146–48, 151, 163, 173,
    180–86, 207, 208, 210, 214, 218, 225, 226,
    228–30, 251, 257, 258
    Order of Ontario, 165
Ontario Society of Artists, 89
Opening of Parliament, see Parliament
Order of Canada, see Canadian Hours System
Order of Merit, see Canadian Honours System
Order of Merit of the Police Forces, see
    Canadian Honours System
Order of Military Merit, see Canadian
    Honours System
Osborn, Captain, Henry, 106

Pachter, Charles, 104
Page, The Honourable J. Percy, 222

Parliament Buildings, 62, 192, 224, 228, 234, 230
    Parliament of Canada, 15, 19, 45 , 49, 51–53,
        55, 57, 62, 63, 67, 69, 73, 74, 76–78,
        82, 97, 180, 192, 207, 210, 224, 234,
        240–42, 247, 248 , 253, 258, 260, 264
    Corbels, 230
    Dissolution of Parliament, 258
    House of Commons, 15, 19, 45, 53, 57,
        58, 62, 63, 65, 67, 69, 73, 78, 97, 210,
        211, 221, 242, 247, 248, 259–62
    Opening of Parliament
    Parliamentary democracy, 69, 262
    Prorogation of Parliament (208), 52, 53
    Senate, 15, 19, 49, 58, 62, 63, 69, 73,
        77, 78, 81, 97, 133, 234, 240, 242,
        248, 250, 252, 253, 260, 264
Particelli, Michel, 82
Paterson, The Honourable Walter, 214
Patricia, Princess (daughter of Prince Arthur,
    Duke of Connaught), 230
Princess Patricia's Own Canadian Light
    Infantry, 230
Patron Scout of Canada, see Governors General
Pearkes, The Honourable George Randolph,
    118, 225
Pearson, The Right Honourable Lester B.,
    157, 161
Pekisko, Alberta, 192, 193, 227, 228
Penfield, Colonel Dr. Wilder, 161
Peerages granted by the British Crown:
    In consultation with the Canadian
        Government, 212
    Without consultation with the Canadian
        Government, 212
Personal Canadian Flag:

Of the Duke of Cambridge, 191
Of the Prince of Wales, 195
Of the Queen, 74, 191, 222
Peterborough, Ontario, 110, 118
Peters, The Honourable Steve, 185
Philip, Prince (Duke of Edinburgh), 110, 113,
    115, 146, 180–84, 208, 216, 219, 249
    As admiral, 151
    As air commodore-in-chief, 151
    As colonel-in-chief, 147
    As honorary commodore, 151
    Duke of Edinburgh's Award, 114
Plains of Abraham (Quebec), 31, 92
Point, The Honourable Steven Lewis, 96, 98,
    127, 218
Premier, 58, 59, 65, 97, 258, 259, 261–64
Prime Minister, 46, 57–59, 63, 65, 67, 73, 74,
    81, 248, 258, 259, 261, 262, 263
Prince Edward Island, Province of (formerly St.
    John's Island, 16, 19, 30, 34, 36, 39, 41, 68,
    78, 97, 100, 115, 116, 124, 148, 152, 168,
    181, 192, 214, 216, 218, 220, 226, 251, 258
    Order of Prince Edward Island, 166
    Prince Edward Island Regiment, 150, 152
Province of Quebec, 37
Province House, Prince Edward Island, 16
Provincial Orders, see Canadian Honours
    System
Provincial Parliaments:
    Legislative Assembly of Alberta, 253
    Legislative Assembly of British
        Columbia, 253
    Legislative Assembly of Manitoba, 253
    Legislative Assembly of New Brunswick,
        78, 253

House of Assembly (Newfoundland and
    Labrador), 64
Legislative Assembly of Nova Scotia, 38,
    78, 253
Legislative Assembly of Ontario, 253
Legislative Assembly of Prince Edward
    Island, 253
National Assembly (Quebec), 64, 69, 97,
    253, 253
Legislative Assembly of Saskatchewan, 253

Quebec, Province of, 19, 27, 30, 32–34, 37, 41, 42,
    51, 60, 64, 69, 89, 89, 95, 98, 99, 101–03, 116,
    118, 146, 147, 162–64, 168, 182, 190, 208,
    211, 217, 220, 223, 243, 251, 257, 258, 264
    Agricultural Merit Awards, 162
    Act Respecting the National Assembly
        (1983), 69
    L'Ordre national du Québec, 164
Quebec Act (1774), 32
Quebec City, 27, 31, 33, 34, 36, 49, 97, 118,
    128, 162, 180, 182, 192, 197, 208, 216,
    224, 226, 234, 253
Quebec Civil Code, 226
Quebec Conference (1864), 41–42, 180
Quebec Conferences (1943 and 1944), see
    Second World War
Queen Anne and the Four Indian Kings
    (1710), 131–32
Queen Anne's Chapel, Mohawk Valley, 138, 140
Queen Anne's War (1702–13), 28
Queen Elizabeth Way (Ontario), 107, 109, 226
Queen's Arms in Right:
    Of Canada, 71, 72
    Of Saskatchewan, 73

Queen's Colours:
    Argyll and Sutherland Highlanders of
        Canada, 144
    Halton Regional Force, 107
Queen's Personal Honours, 159, 16
    Royal Victorian Chain, 161
    Royal Victorian Order, 161
    Royal Victorian Medal, 161
Queen's Privy Council, 58–59, 62, 143
    Cabinet, 19, 38, 57–60, 62, 65, 73, 143,
        259, 261–63
Queen's Rangers (1st American Regiment), 224

Raleigh, Sir Walter, 25
Ramon John Hnatyshyn Cup, see Canadian
    International Dragon Boat Festival
Rankin Inlet, Nunavut, 123
Red Crow, Chief (Blood Tribe), 218
Reid, The Honourable Marion, 220
Representative government, 20, 30
Remembrance Day, 152
    First poppy, 152
Republic, 34, 47, 107, 203, 263
    American republic, 34
Reserve Powers of the Crown, 65–67
Resolute Bay, Northwest Territories, 196
Responsible government, 19, 20, 36–38, 57,
    58, 60, 63, 66, 143, 208, 263
Revolutionary War, see American Revolution
Richard Dimbelby Lecture, 195
Richard, Maurice "Rocket," 216
Richelieu, Cardinal (Armand-Jean du Plessis),
    27, 237
Rideau Hall (Government House) (Ottawa),
    86, 92, 157, 174, 194, 224, 225, 259

Chancellery of Honours, 174
    Fountain of Hope, 224
Robitaille, The Honourable Théodore, 89
Roosevelt, President Franklin D., 33, 217
Routhier, Judge Adolph-Basile, 89
Royal 22e Régiment (the Van Doos), 92, 256
Royal American Regiment (60th Regiment of
    Foot), 134
Royal Arms of Canada, 60, 222, see also
    Queen's Arms in Right of Canada
Royal Arms of New France, 25
Royal Assent, 42, 49, 63, 67–69, 82, 97, 99,
    242, 248, 263
Royal Canadian Academy, 89, 120
Royal Canadian Air Cadets, 151
Royal Canadian Air Force, 222
Royal Canadian Golf Association, 208
Royal Canadian Heritage Trust, 253
Royal Canadian Mint, 154
Royal Canadian Mounted Police (RCMP), 107, 181
Royal Canadian Naval College, 219
Royal Canadian Naval Sailing Association, 151
Royal Canadian Navy, 76, 183
Royal Canadian Regiment Battle Group, 1st
    Battalion, 85
Royal Canoes, 110
Royal Charter:
Hudson's Bay Company (1670), 28
    International Scouting Movement, 91
    Nova Scotia (1621), 213
    Université Laval (1852), 208
    University of King's College (1756), 209
Royal Collection (artworks), 132
Royal Commission on Aboriginal Peoples
    (1996), 133

Royal Commission on National Development
    in the Arts, Letters and Sciences, *see*
    Massey Commission
Royal cypher, 229, 250
Royal Grant, 39
Royal Flight, 230
Royal Fusiliers, 7th Regiment of Foot, 34
Royal Manitoba Winter Fair, 228
Royal Patrons, 111–13
Royal Prefix, 107, 108, 110–111, 208
Royal Prerogative, 65–67, 97, 153, 169, 245, 262–63
Royal Proclamation (1763), 31–33, 57,
    132–34, *see also* George III
Royal Proclamation (1749), 216
Royal Regiment of Canada, The, 149
Royal Regiment of Canadian Artillery, The, 151
Royal Roads Military College (Colwood,
    British Columbia), 219
Royal Salute, 214
Royal St. John's Regatta (Newfoundland and
    Labrador), 111, 208
Royal Society of Canada, 89, 120
Royal Standard, 215
Royal Styles and Titles Act (1953), 20, 50
Royal Tours, 179–184
    By Duke and Duchess of Cambridge, 19,
        180, 199
    By the Queen and Prince Philip, 180–83,
        199, 219, 230
    By other members of the Royal family,
        184, 189, 192, 217, 219, 230
    Royal Tour of 1939, 49, 107
Royal trains, 219
Royal Victorian Chain, 161, 211, *see* Queen`s
    Personal Honours

Royal Victorian Medal, 161, *see* Queen's
    Personal Honours
Royal Victorian Order, 161, *see* Queen's
    Personal Honours
Royal Warrant, 221
Royal William (steamship), 216
Royal Winter Agricultural Fair (Toronto),
    195, 228
Rupert, Prince (Count Palatine of the
    Rhine, Duke of Bavaria, 1st Duke of
    Cumberland, 1st Earl of Holderness), 28
Rupert's Land, 43–44

St. Jean Baptiste Society of Quebec, 89
St. John's, Newfoundland and Labrador, 95,
    148, 181, 182, 197
St. John's Island, *see* Prince Edward Island
St. Louis of France (Louis IX of France,
    1226–1270), 54–55
St. Mark's Anglican Church (Port Hope), 218
St. Paul's Anglican Church (Halifax), 216
St. Pierre and Miquelon, 31
Saskatchewan, Province of, 19, 28, 44, 76, 94, 97,
    98, 103, 115, 116,118, 136, 148, 163, 164,
    181–83, 189, 207, 208, 211, 251, 253, 258
    Saskatchewan Order of Merit, 164
Sauvé, The Right Honourable Jeanne, 85, 118,
    120, 239
    Jeanne Sauvé Cup, *see* National Ringette
        League
    Sauvé Foundation, 120
Sewell, Jonathan, 36, 131
Schreyer, The Right Honourable Edward, 93
Schuyler, Peter, 131
Scouts Canada:

Chief Scout Award, 91
Queen's Venturer Award, 91
Second World War, 117, 152, 220, 232
Lancaster bombers 152
Quebec Conferences (1943 and 1944), 217
Secord, Laura, 192
Secretaries and private secretaries, 246
Secretary to the Governor General, 174, 187
Canadian Secretary to the Queen, 71, 159, 179, 243
Sergeant-at-Arms, 78, 246–48
Seven Years' War, see French and Indian Wars (1756–1763)
Simcoe, The Honourable John Graves, 33, 118, 218, 224, 228
Simmie, Allyson M., 61
Simpson, Wallis (Duchess of Windsor), 227, 228
Sioui, Chief Konrad (Wendat), 128
Slave Lake, Alberta, 183
Smith, Arnold (Commonwealth), 210
Smith, Dr. David, 79
Sovereign Council (1663), 27
Speaker, 248
Of the House of Commons, 58, 63, 68, 210, 211, 221, 247, 248
Of the provincial legislatures, 68, 70,185, 218, 220, 247
Of the Senate, 58, 78, 248, 250, 252
Stanley, The Honourable George, 214
Stanley Cup, see National Hockey League
Stanley of Preston, Lord (Sir Frederick Stanley, Baron of Preston), 90, 118, 119, 121, 239

Stanley Park (Vancouver), 119
Statute of Westminster (1931), see British Parliament
Steinhauer, The Honourable Ralph G., 224
Sullivan, Sir Arthur, 89
Supreme Court of Canada, 51, 62, 77, 131, 133
Symons, Professor Thomas H.B., 13, 18, 20

Taylor, Charles, 17
Tecumseh (Shawnee Chief), 135
Territorial Legislatures:
Legislative Assembly of the Northwest Territories, 61, 253
Legislative Assembly of Nunavut, 61, 253
Legislative Assembly of Yukon, 253
Thirteen Colonies (British North American), 32, 33, 133, 134, 217
Thompson, Private Richard Rowland, 210
Thompson, The Right Honourable Sir John, 217
Tilley, The Honourable Sir Samuel Leonard, 42, 211
Treaties:
Treaty of Paris (1763), 31
Treaty of Separation (1783), 217
Treaty of Suza (1629), 213
Treaty of Utrecht (1713), 28–29
Treaty Days (Crown and First Nations), 136–37
Trudeau, The Right Honourable Pierre Elliot, 51
Tweedsmuir, Lord (John Buchan, 1st Baron Tweedsmuir), 86, 139, 157, 187, 239

Union Act (1840), 37
United Empire Loyalist, Loyalists (UEL), 32, 221
Armorial Bearings, 32

United Nations, 197, 201
United States of America, 18, 19, 34, 41, 44, 49, 54, 73, 83, 134, 187, 210, 217, 220, 224, 230
Université Laval (Quebec City), 208
University of King's College, 209, *see also* Royal Charter
Upper Canada, Province of, 33, 37, 134, 135, 138, 214, 216, 224, 226, 228
Upper and Lower Canada Rebellions (1837–1838), 37, 229, 230, 257
Usher of the Black Rod in the Senate, see Black Rod, 71, 78, 241–43

Vance, Jonathan, 89
Vancouver, British Columbia, 49, 119, 121, 124, 147, 181, 182
Vancouver Island, Colony of, 28, 39, 134, 217
    House of Assembly, 134
Vanier, The Right Honourable Georges-Philéas, 85, 118, 120, 122, 157, 220, 239
    Vanier Cup, *see* Canadian Interuniversity Sport football
    Vanier Institute of the Family, 120
Verelst, Jan, 132
Vice-Regal Tours, 184–86
Victoria, British Columbia, 116, 197, 141, 151, 181, 182, 197
Victoria, Queen, 34, 39, 42, 44, 108, 115, 116, 128, 161, 162, 208, 210, 216, 216–18, 226, 228, 230, 234, 235, 264
    Diamond Jubilee, 217
    Victoria Day, 210, 264
Victoria Cross (Canada), *see* Canadian Victoria Cross

Victoria Cross, 155, 225
Victorian Order of Nurses (VON), 217
Vimy Memorial (France), 143, 145, 226
Vimy Ridge, *see* First World War

War of 1812 (1812–1814), 14, 36, 135, 141, 192, 215
    Battle of Moraviantown, 135
War of the Spanish Succession, *see* Queen Anne's War
Washington, George, 31
Waterdown District High School (Ontario), 21
    Student Parliament, 21
Wendat First Nation, 128
Wessex, Countess of (Sophie Rhys-Jones), as colonel-in-chief, 148
Weston, The Honourable Hilary, 65
Wheeler-Bennett, J.W., 192
William IV, King of Great Britain, 190, 214, 216, 218, 235
    As Prince, 190, 214
William, Prince (Duke of Cambridge), 104, 122, 151, 184, 197–99
Willingdon, Lord (Freeman Freeman-Thomas, 1st Marquess of Willingdon, Viscount Willingdon of Ratton), 46, 118 187, 237
    Willingdon Cup, *see* Golf Canada Championship
Wolfe, Major-General James P., 31
Worobetz, The Honourable Dr. Stephen, 207

Yukon, Territory of, 28, 44, 118, 253, 258

ABOUT THE AUTHOR

Nathan Tidridge was awarded the Queen's Golden Jubilee Medal for his fifteen years of volunteer support in the education of Canadians on the role of the Crown. He teaches Canadian history and government at Waterdown District High School and was awarded the Premier's Award for Teaching Excellence (Teacher of the Year) in 2008. In 2011 he was awarded the Charles Baillie Award for Excellence in Secondary School Teaching by Queen's University. Tidridge lives in Carlisle, Ontario, with his wife Christine and daughter Sophie.

OF RELATED INTEREST

Royal Tours 1786–2010
Home to Canada
by Arthur Bousfield and Gary Toffoli

978-155488009

$24.99

Royal Tours 1786–2010 is a penetrating look at the tours of eleven royals who were or would be monarchs, viceroys, and commanders-in-chief of Canada. Leaving California in 1983 to tour British Columbia, Queen Elizabeth II said she was "going home to Canada." Since its pioneer days, the Royal family has made the country home through tours of public service, naval, and military duty, and residence. Beautifully illustrated, featuring photos from the June/July 2010 tour of the Queen, *Royal Tours 1786–2010* is a captivating look at how these tours shaped Canada and the royals themselves, with an eye for the significant, interesting, and humorous.

Canadian Symbols of Authority

Maces, Chains, and Rods of Office

by Corinna Pike and Christopher McCreery

978-1554889013

$60.00

The first book to examine the various parliamentary maces, rods, badges, and chains of office used throughout Canada, *Canadian Symbols of Authority* details how these devices are used at every level of government, emphasizing how, like the Crown itself, they embody continuity in an ever-changing world. Symbols of authority are not only emblems of democracy and authority, but they are part of the diverse heraldic and artistic heritage of Canada. From the Great Maces of the Senate and House of Commons to the Chancellor's Chain of the Order of Canada and Baton of the Chief Herald, the development of Canada's symbols of authority encompasses the past 250 years of Canadian history. Richly illustrated, this book is the most comprehensive study yet undertaken of the origins, history, and development of parliamentary maces.

DUNDURN
www.dundurn.com

What did you think of this book?
Visit www.dundurn.com for reviews, videos, updates, and more!